God's Strategic Plan

Robert V. Fullerton, CPA, MBA.

ISBN-13: 978-1497337817
ISBN-10: 149733781X

Author's Contact Information:
2119 Water Mill Ct.
Buford, GA. 30519, USA.

Email: rfullerton@christiancfo.com

Websites: www.christiancfo.com; www.rvfcfo.com

DEDICATION

This book is dedicated to my darling wife Jacqueline, for her love and encouragement, and for her faith in God to hear when I could not, and to believe when I did not.

CONTENTS

ACKNOWLEDGMENTS

We sometimes go through periods of trial in our lives, when things seem far more challenging than we can handle, and when we question the meaning and purpose of our lives. This book was written at such a time in mine. I thank God for His grace, patience, love, and forgiveness; and for enabling me to write this book.

I wish to express my gratitude to the following people, who not only helped with the production of this book, but provided support and advice when I needed it.

To my darling daughter Chloe, and my nephew Nigel Assam, for editing my work, correcting my mistakes, and challenging me to express my thoughts with greater clarity.

To Minister Genny Alvarez for her review of the Scriptural content and doctrinal points of the book.

To my best friends and brothers in the Lord, Mark Teelucksingh and Michael Douglas, for their wisdom, love, advice, and prayers.

To my brothers Angus and Terry for working tirelessly on my behalf.

To all of my family, both Fullertons and Assams, for their love and laughter.

God Bless you all.

CHAPTER 1

THE ORIGIN OF STRATEGIC PLANNING

Few things cause more of a stir in the business world than the hostile takeover of one major corporation by another. Hostile takeovers intrigue us because they are usually the work of a cunning mastermind, developing and implementing strategic moves in secret, catching everyone, including the intended victim, completely unawares.

Corporate takeovers provide excellent material for Hollywood film-makers. Movies such as "Wall Street" (1987) and its sequel "Wall Street: Money Never Sleeps" (2010) take us behind the scenes to examine the human drama and the brilliant strategy that are often required for success. While hostile corporate takeovers have been a relatively new means of business expansion, the practice of seizing ownership by craft and stealth is not a recent phenomenon at all. *It has actually been around since the beginning of time.*

My interest in Strategic Planning grew out of my training and experience as a business professional. Superior corporate strategy is often what distinguishes successful businesses from the ones that fail (or fall victim to takeovers), and in today's competitive market it is almost impossible for any business to grow profitably without a sound strategic plan.

Planning is such a critical aspect of effective management, that every business school teaches it, every CEO practices it and there are hundreds of books written by experts explaining what it is and how it is best implemented. I have found at least a dozen different definitions of strategic planning written in textbooks, articles and business papers. The following is one of the simpler more understandable versions, which is found in the Online Business Dictionary:

"Strategic Planning is the systematic process of envisioning a desired future and translating this vision into broadly defined objectives and a sequence of steps to achieve them."

A strategic plan is simply a defined process by which we achieve the objectives we envisage. It is all about knowing what we want and figuring out how to get it. Formulating and executing strategy is an important part of competitive advantage, and businesses of all sizes (yes, *small ones too*) must devote time and effort to proper planning in order to survive and succeed.

But where did the practice of planning strategy originate? Who wrote the first strategic plan? Research suggests that formal planning emerged as a business management tool sometime in the 1960s and became popular in the 1980s as business scholars and practitioners developed new methods and applications.

Man's ability to apply strategic thinking to achieve desired objectives was probably first used centuries before that on the field of human conflict. At some point in man's history, people began to live together in family units. Groups of families developed alliances for security purposes, or to pool resources to hunt game or grow crops. This eventually led to associations of connected families in tribes, with tribes eventually growing and expanding their domains to form nations.

Somewhere along the line, a disagreement would have broken out between two or more early family groups or tribes. Who knows what sparked the first tribal conflict. Maybe it was as a result of a dispute over some scarce resource like food or water. Maybe it was over an insult, or the encroachment of one tribe on a rival's protected territory.

Whatever the cause, the first tribal war was probably won by brute force, with very little thought given to battle strategy or coordination of effort. Man soon realized that victory in battle depended not just on superior numbers, physical strength, and fighting skill, but on careful planning. Human history clearly shows that man has applied strategic planning for military purposes, long before it was adapted to business use. It is likely that the first formal strategic plan was developed by some ancient tribal leader attempting to come up with a plan to overcome an enemy.

I believe however that this process started even further back in time than business scholars suggest. I submit that the origin of strategic planning actually pre-dates man's tribal conflicts and business pursuits and that deliberate strategy has a significant role to play in ultimately determining the fate of the human race.

There is evidence to suggest that an ancient battle, which started long before time as we know it began, continues to rage on today, unseen by the eyes of men. This battle often spills over into the human arena as the opposing parties implement different strategic initiatives over time.

The effects of this unseen conflict have far more serious consequences for the future of mankind than any other modern day issue engaging our attention, including concerns such as the level of the national debt, global warming or conflicts among nations with nuclear power.

To understand more about this strategic contest and how it affects us all, we need to go back, way back, to a time *before* man walked the earth.

CHAPTER 2

IN THE BEGINNING

In our introduction to strategic planning we discovered that man applied strategic thinking to military pursuits long before it was adapted for business purposes. In fact, modern day business decision makers often study the exploits of successful military leaders for insights and ideas that can be applied in the corporate world.

One of the more notable instances in which this has been done is the adaptation of the writings of Chinese military leader, General Sun Tzu, to business strategy. General Sun Tzu is said to have lived about 600 years BC, and his dissertation on warfare is considered one of the greatest handbooks on military strategy ever written. The General's writings have been adapted to corporate management, and today in business libraries you can find a wide selection of books by various authors with titles beginning with *"The Art of War for.."* managers, business executives, sales and marketing, career building, business women, and so on.

While General Sun Tzu's writings provide valuable advice on addressing military and business issues, their application is specific and limited mainly to those fields. What most of us desperately need in today's chaotic world is not insights on military strategy, but a reference manual providing information to help us deal with life's constant challenges. We need guidance and advice not just on business and finance, but on a wide range of personal, emotional, psychological, moral and spiritual issues. To that end, I submit that the Bible fits the bill perfectly. As a reference manual for daily living, it addresses every strategic issue known to man. Not only is it a powerful source of inspiration and guidance for life's challenges, it is also the greatest and most comprehensive book on strategic planning *ever written*.

Imbedded in the pages of scripture are practical insights on subjects such as business and money management, physical and spiritual warfare, conflict resolution, love, marriage, health, parenting, ethics, and countless others. But as important as these issues are, the Bible is truly amazing because of its primary assertion.

The Bible makes the astounding claim first and foremost, to be the revelation of God's strategic purpose for the human race.

It sets out to make the case that God exists, that He has a specific plan for human beings and that He has set in motion a series of strategic initiatives to achieve His divine objective on our behalf. As a student of strategic planning, I find it hard to resist examining this assertion further. *If* God does have a deliberate agenda that involves us personally, then that becomes the most important consideration for each of us, since it would address issues relating to the way we live, the decisions we make now, and our ultimate destiny. So, let us go back in time and peer behind the scenes of some of the events recorded in the Bible, to determine if there is a strategic agenda imbedded in Scripture. To do this, we must start at the very beginning of the beginning, which incidentally is not found in the book of Genesis, but in the book of Isaiah.

> "How you are fallen from heaven O Lucifer, son of the morning! How you are cut down to the ground, who weakened the nations! For you have said in your heart: I will ascend into heaven, I will exalt my throne above the stars of God: I will also sit on the mount of the congregation, on the farthest sides of the north: I will ascend above the heights of the clouds; I will be like the most High."
> (Isaiah 14:12-14)

This account in the book of Isaiah of the secret thoughts of one of God's angels Lucifer, and his lust for power and glory, is also described by the prophet Ezekiel.

> Your heart was lifted up because of your beauty, you corrupted your wisdom for the sake of your splendor; I will cast you to the ground, I will lay you before kings, that they might gaze at you.
> (Ezekiel 28:17)

In these two passages of Scripture, we find the answer to the question of the origin of conflict and the root cause of war in heavenly places as well as on the earth. All of the wars ever fought in the history of mankind, and all of the turmoil and evil we see in the world today, have their genesis right here. Isaiah and Ezekiel tell us that Lucifer, "son of the morning", potentially the brightest and most talented of all of God's creations, became convinced of his own greatness and concluded that he and not God, deserved to sit on the Throne of heaven. This evil idea most likely developed over a period of time as Lucifer began to first admire his own beauty and glory and then to secretly worship himself. This led to the conviction that he was as glorious as God and therefore just as deserving to sit on the Throne. Lucifer's obsession with God's Throne and his desire to own it for himself, became his primary strategic goal. To achieve this objective, he knew he would have to come up with a really brilliant plan and so, he sat down (not literally) to consider his options.

Lucifer's options:

1. Power sharing: I suspect that Lucifer would not have objected (at least initially) to being equal with God if this offer was made to him ("I would be *like* the most High"). The Apostle Paul, in explaining the process by which Jesus humbled himself to walk among men, said that Jesus: "who, being in the form of God, did not consider it robbery to be equal with God, but made Himself of no reputation, taking the form of a bondservant and coming in the likeness of men" (Philippians 2:6-7). Lucifer desperately wanted to take possession of the very thing that Jesus was prepared to relinquish: equality with God. Power sharing of God's Throne is however a divine impossibility because there can be only one God, in the same way that a kingdom can be ruled by only one king.

2. Have God impeached and force Him to abdicate the Throne. Just as the Constitution is the foundation of our country's laws, God's word operates as the law of heaven. If God could be found guilty of breaking His own word, then He would lose His divine right to the Throne, in the same way that any president

who broke the law of the land could be impeached and removed from office. God has made Himself subject to His own word (Psalm 138:2) and if Satan could provoke or manipulate Him to act emotionally and not righteously, then he could open the door to a valid claim. We will explore this in more detail later on.

3. Take the Throne by force.

Since there was no apparent basis on which to impeach God and power sharing was not open for discussion, the only option left for Lucifer was to plan and execute a coup. Lucifer knew, as do all military dictators, that a successful coup depended on the support of the army. For this to work, he needed to get the support of as many of God's angels as he could, and this became a top tactical priority. Whether Satan canvassed the angels secretly or openly before God is not clear. However, as soon as he felt that he had the backing of a sufficient number of rebels he executed his evil plan and launched the attack.

> And war broke out in heaven: Michael and his angels fought against the dragon: and the dragon fought, but they did not prevail, nor was a place found for them in heaven any longer. So the great dragon was cast out, that serpent of old, called the Devil and Satan, who deceives the whole world; he was cast to the earth, and his angels were cast out with him.
> (Revelation 12: 7-9)

The sequence of events so far is in two parts. Isaiah and Ezekiel describe Lucifer's transformation from a glorious being to the epitome of evil, and his insane aspiration to take God's throne. The book of Revelation then relates the account of the ensuing war between the forces of God and evil, Lucifer's defeat and his expulsion from heaven. The book of Luke now connects the final dot for us:

> "Then the seventy returned again with joy, saying, Lord, even the demons are subject unto us in Your name. And he said unto them, I saw Satan fall like lightning from heaven. Behold, I give you authority to trample on serpents and scorpions, and over all the power of the enemy and nothing shall by any means hurt you."
> (Luke 10:17-19)

In this account in Luke, we are told of a time when Jesus gave His disciples authority over demons and sent them on a mission to cast these spirits out of tormented people. On their return the disciples were elated at their success. Jesus in commenting on their victories, made the astounding statement: *"I saw Satan fall like lightning from heaven."* There are two things we glean from this:

1. Jesus made a direct connection between the presence of demonic forces on the earth and the expulsion of Satan from heaven. It appears that the angelic beings that were cast out with Satan are now living in and among men on the earth. If I were one of these disciples, I certainly would have been very concerned by this revelation. "What Lord, do you mean that the demons we were casting out are connected to Satan, *the Satan, the most evil of all beings?"* Jesus immediately provides the ultimate assurance to His disciples (which extends to us today as well): "Behold, *I* give you authority over them, and *nothing* can by any means hurt you".

2. The other amazing thing Jesus tells His disciples is: "I *saw* Satan fall." My question would have been, "Lord, do you mean that you were *there* when this

happened?" As we shall see in the coming chapters, not only was Jesus there when this feud began, but He is the key to how it ends.

There are some important aspects of Lucifer's strategy and God's response to the plot to overthrow Him, which we must examine further. Consider the following:

1) How was Lucifer able to persuade the angels in heaven, who stood in the presence of God, to rebel against The Almighty?

The answer is that he was and is the great deceiver and manipulator. His main strategy is to offer his intended victim something that he thinks cannot be refused. He does this by studying his target to figure out which buttons to press to achieve his strategic objective.

In the account of Matthew 4:9, Lucifer (aka Satan) attempted to get Jesus to bow down and worship him by first showing Jesus all the kingdoms of the world and then offering to give them to Him in exchange for a pledge of allegiance (Matt: 4:9). Satan believed that Jesus came to earth to attempt to set up a kingdom among men, so why not make it easy for Him? "Bow down and worship me, Jesus, and it's all yours."

That may also have been his tactic with the angels; make them offers of individual position in the post-coup order in exchange for their support in overthrowing God. This was his approach to Adam and Eve in the Garden of Eden (as we shall see), then with Jesus in the wilderness, and you better believe he uses that same tactic on man today. Although Satan failed in his bid to seize God's Throne (which was the very first hostile takeover ever attempted), he is still pursuing a secondary agenda among men. His revised plan is to persuade as many as he can to join him and his demonic forces in an on-going rebellion against God. His approach and offer are usually so subtle that many are often unaware that we have signed on to his agenda and have positioned ourselves against the will of God. It is this world-wide rebellion against God that is responsible for the rampant evil we find among men up to this very time. This is the unseen battle taking place in our midst, and anyone who takes a stand for God becomes a target for Satan and is subject to attack. None of us is capable of matching wits with the deceiver in our own strength. The only way we can turn him away is to realize that we are in a battle and follow Jesus' example. Scripture gives us the basis for repelling the attacks of the devil. The process involves *submitting* and then *resisting*.

"Therefore submit to God. Resist the devil and he will flee from you".
(James 4:7)

2. Why did God allow Lucifer to attempt a coup in the first place? Was He taken by surprise?

Surely God knows all and must have seen the evil developing in Lucifer's heart. God must also have observed Lucifer planting the seeds of rebellion among the angels. Why did He not intervene to stop Lucifer in his tracks? I believe that God grants everyone, including the angels, the free will to serve Him, if they choose to. God knows all things and could have stopped Lucifer and the angels before they acted. But to do that would have been to deny them the freedom to choose to live in obedience to God or to rebel.

Once God gives us the freedom to choose, He will not stop us from exercising that right if we insist, regardless of the consequences. Although God gave the Israelites very specific laws and commandments, He never *demanded* their obedience but always allowed them to chose to voluntarily do what they knew to be right. The following is one of His many such appeals to them (and to us):

> "I call heaven and earth as witness today against you, that I have set before you life and death, blessing and cursing; therefore choose life that both you and your descendants may live."
> (Deuteronomy 30:19)

Yes, God does impose consequences for disobedience as any good parent would, but He will never force us to obey or love Him because He will not make slaves of men or angels.

3: Why didn't God obliterate Lucifer and his rebels immediately?

Lucifer's attempt to overthrow the Kingdom of God by violent means is arguably the most serious act of treason ever committed. One would think that the punishment for this crime would be both swift and severe. The sentence imposed by God, banishment from heaven and exile to earth does not appear to fit the crime from man's perspective.

Treason is in many countries a capital offense. History has shown that the usual fate of a failed coup leader is capture, swift trial (if he is lucky enough to *get* a trial) and immediate execution. Why was Lucifer's punishment so apparently lenient? Why was he not dealt with more harshly than this? Was God not entitled to strip him of all power and immediately confine him to everlasting chains? What crime could he *ever* commit that would be more grievous than this?

As we will see later, Lucifer's exile to earth was not a miscalculation by God but a major part of His brilliant strategy. This is not the end but rather the beginning of a long war where planning and strategy would prove critical. The scene is now set for a classic showdown. On the one hand, we have Almighty God, the Righteous Judge who sits on the Throne, and on the other we have the expelled foe, beaten but not yet defeated, full of hate, and bent on revenge. The battle and our focus, now shift from the angelic realm in the heavens to the earth, where God has created a strange new being, called "man."

We will next consider how we all became embroiled in this conflict between spiritual authorities and how earth became the battlefield.

CHAPTER 3

EARTH, THE BATTLEFIELD

The Bible is sometimes described (usually by those unfamiliar with its contents), as "a book of stories and myths" and therefore not to be taken seriously or literally. It is true that many of the books of the Bible contain accounts of supernatural acts that don't fit into our modern-day experience.

We live in a world where technology drives our lives and defines our reality. Things are real and make sense to us if we can explain them in the context of existing technology. While I don't personally understand the science that enables a fifty ton aircraft to fly, or that makes video conferencing possible, I accept these modern marvels as real because I have experienced them first hand, and somewhere out there are scientists who invented them and know how they work. The consensus in today's world seems to be that anything with a scientific basis is accepted as valid and anything that science is unable to explain is deemed a myth. As a result, a book that relates accounts of the parting of the Red Sea by a man holding a stick, a big boat sitting somewhere on the top of Mount Ararat, miraculous healing of the sick, or raising of the dead, is either mistaken or an invention of man's imagination.

This is why many today believe that the miracles described in scripture are exaggerated accounts of normal events, distorted as they were passed down from one generation of "storytellers" to another. Sadly that seems to be a common view held by a large number of people. Satan is also working on a plan of his own to distort reality for man. For example there is a rapidly growing fascination with the resurrection of the dead as entertainment, in the form of movies about vampires, zombies and the "undead".

In my opinion the devil is at work to deceive, using a sort of reverse psychology on the viewing public. It is obvious that what we see on the screen is the product of creative film-making, visual effects, and clever make-up. What is not so obvious is the subtle message being conveyed, that the resurrection of the dead is a movie myth and therefore not real. Satan is targeting the minds of the younger, more impressionable generation since this is where this type of "programming" (very apt word) seems to be aimed. If Satan can condition our teens and young adults to accept the walking dead as good PG-13 entertainment, then their version of reality will be that the resurrection of the dead is folklore. Each passing generation that feeds on this deception is less likely to accept the resurrection of Jesus as an eternal truth. Subtle, but effective.

Satan is a counterfeiter. I submit that his ideas for mummies came from the image we get in John 11:44 of Jesus calling Lazarus out of the tomb, wrapped in his burial clothes. While the practice of mummifying had been around for centuries before Lazarus was born, his is the first description we have of one actually walking out of a grave covered from head to foot in burial clothes. This, in my opinion, is where the idea for the image portrayed on the screen came from. Interestingly, the hard faced intimidating TV vampires of old, played by such scary actors as Peter Cushing and Christopher Lee, have been replaced by very attractive, very charming young actors and the new vampire stories are built around young romance, bonds of friendship and sacrificial love. No longer does Hollywood portray the vampire as a sinister villain, he/she is now a hero and a heartthrob. It seems that it is not only man who uses science to define reality, the devil has gotten into the act as well.

The world we live in is now divided into two distinct camps; those who believe the Bible to be a collection of stories inspired by man's imagination, and those who believe that it is the revelation of the will of a strategic God, who acts with purpose, and who is not governed by the rules of science. The deciding factor in my opinion is the supernatural ability of the words contained in this book, **to change the lives of people,** thousands of years after they were written.

As we embrace the truth of God's word, we soon realize that Biblical accounts are not random stories invented by men, *but staging points in time*, which all focus attention on a very real, ongoing dispute between two opposing forces.

Scripture presents itself *as fact* and what greets the reader at the start of Genesis, is not "Once upon a time" or, "In a kingdom far, far away", but the profound statement: "In the beginning, God.." Genesis provides a factual account of how everything around us was created and science is apparently just beginning to catch on to this truth.

It is now believed that the so-called "God-particle" or the Higgs boson, (named after Nobel prize-winning physicist Peter Higgs) suggests that the universe was actually created in a specific split second of time, before which nothing existed. Sounds like the science guys are slowly coming up to speed. The opening statement in the Bible is:

"In the beginning God created the heaven and the earth." (Genesis 1:1)

Then, rather than logically going on to explain more about heaven's creation since it was mentioned first, the text bypasses heaven altogether and immediately begins to explain the creation of the earth. By focusing on the creation of the earth and then of man, Genesis sets the scene to introduce the three main characters involved in God's strategic plan as they interact for the very first time. Let us examine this inter-relationship from Satan's point of view.

In our previous chapter, we learned that Lucifer, now called Satan, was expelled from the presence of God, kicked out of heaven and exiled to the earth. Sitting as an outcast in his place of exile, Satan has time to brood and contemplate his next steps. The two overwhelming emotions he feels at this point are hatred for God and an intense lust for revenge. While pride, greed and resentment were his motivation for the attempted coup, hatred for God and a desire for revenge become his new obsession. So, what are his strategic options at this stage?

1) Exact revenge by striking back at God directly. Not a good idea. Satan's failed attempt to seize God's throne demonstrates that this approach is doomed to fail. God is all powerful and simply cannot be overcome.

2) Exact revenge on God by striking back at His angels. This is the old terrorist tactic: if I can't hurt you, I will hurt someone you love. Satan is well aware that this plan is also

unlikely to succeed. God's remaining loyal angels are simply not to be trifled with. Michael and his crew are very formidable, powerful warriors and know how to handle themselves in battle. They were not easy targets and attacking them directly would be futile.

Satan apparently does not have very many workable options at this time. What he really needs is to find an easier, more vulnerable target, one that was not as powerful as the angels in heaven, and is not constantly in the presence of God. **But who?** While still contemplating his next move, Satan observes that God is busy at work, doing something unusual on the earth.

> Then God said, "Let Us make man in Our image, according to Our likeness;" And the Lord God formed man of the dust of the ground, and breathed into his nostrils the breath of life; and man became a living being.   (Genesis 1:26-2:7)

To Satan and also to the angels in heaven, the creation of man as a living being was both fascinating and perplexing. "Who is this strange creature? What is his purpose? Why is he created in God's image and likeness? Is man a god, or is he like God?" Clearly man is a physical being and does not have the supernatural power of angels or demons. He also does not seem to be aware of the historical battle between God and Satan. Could this be the soft target that Satan is looking for?

With his curiosity aroused, Satan embarks on a course to study this new creature and evaluate his relationship with God, to see if he could identify any weaknesses that could be exploited. The first thing he discovers is that for no apparent reason, God has given man dominion and authority over the earth, effectively passing legal title on to him. This realization most likely drives Satan into a fit of rage. His defeat by Michael the

Archangel, meant the loss of his bid for dominion in heaven and now, as if to rub salt in his wounds, God gives dominion of the earth to this new creature.

But wait, there is more bad news.

In what appears to be the very first surgery under general anesthetic, God places Adam into a deep sleep, removes one of his ribs and "closed up the flesh in its place" (Genesis 2:21). God then uses this rib to create a mate for Adam and tells the happy couple to multiply and fill the earth *with more people!*

This is Satan's worst nightmare. The very last thing that he needs now, is a whole army of godly men *(this and all other general references to "man" and "men", relate to humans of both sexes),* exercising dominion over him on earth. His greatest fear is that God would give man dominion over him, as punishment for his indiscretions. There is absolutely nothing more terrifying to Satan, than a man or woman standing with godly authority over him. This is why James says that if we resist the devil, he will *"flee"* from us. To flee means to run away in fear and terror, as if pursued. As we shall see later from his encounters with Jesus and the disciples, Satan is terrified of any man or woman who could wield godly authority.

At this point, Satan realizes that he must get the upper hand on Adam before he could reproduce and spread through the earth, so he sets about to find the chinks in Adam's armor. It was soon apparent, that in addition to giving Adam dominion over the earth God seems to be establishing a close and personal relationship with him. God would visit Adam "in the cool of the day" (Genesis 3: 8) to spend time talking with him. Even more than this, God shows open affection for Adam in much the same way that a parent shows affection for a child.

> Out of the ground the Lord God formed every beast of the field and every bird of the air, and brought them unto Adam to see what he would call them. And whatsoever Adam called every living creature, that was its name.
> (Genesis 2:19)

The language in this passage of Scripture suggests that this was more than just a routine exercise to name the animals. God wanted "to see what he would call them." God knows the beginning from the end and knew the names Adam would choose for the animals, even before Adam did. God could also have selected names for the animals Himself and simply told Adam what he should call them. God however wanted Adam to name the animals so he could express his own creativity in a unique and exciting way. This was a special moment in Adam's life and God wanted to be a part of it. "No Adam, that's not a sheep, this one is different. Look closer". "Oh yes Father, I see! Lets call this one goat."

God, the Father:
As parents, we are always excited to see the spark in the eyes of our children, when they experience or achieve something for the first time. We want to be there when they take that first step, say that first word, go on their first visit to the zoo. For Adam and for God, this was such a moment. This was Adam's first trip to the zoo and unlike the rest of us, he got to name all the animals. God has a Father's heart and throughout Scripture, He has always expressed delight in those who draw near to Him as sons and daughters or who honor Him by their faith and obedience.

> And the Lord said unto Satan, "Have you considered my servant Job, that there is none like him on the earth, a blameless and upright man, one who fears God and shuns evil?" (Job1:8)

Now, that is a father's boast, if I ever heard one. With a sense of pride God was saying to Satan, "Check out my boy Job; what an upright and honorable man he is. He obeys my word and trusts me completely. My boy Job is a delight to me, and I am as proud of him, as any father could be!" This is the same declaration that God the Father made about Jesus at the start of His earthly ministry:

> "This is my beloved Son in whom I am well pleased."
> (Matt: 3:17)

God is not shy about showing His affection, or declaring His love for us. In fact, God's way of expressing His love *is to show it.*

> "For God so loved the world that He gave.."
> (John 3:16)

God is loving, giving, and expressive and I am convinced that He did not hide His strong affection for Adam, from Satan. Just as God loved Adam, *Satan hated him with a passion* and wanted to destroy him. There are three motivations for this: **revenge, power and fear.**

Revenge:

God's obvious love for Adam was a source of resentment for Satan as well as provided him with a potential strategic opportunity. Satan wanted revenge and would like nothing better than to strike back at God. Since he could not hurt

God directly maybe he could cause Him some measure of grief by destroying this new creature that He seemed to care so much about.

Power:

Apart from the desire to strike back at God, there was a possible territorial gain to be had by destroying Adam. Satan is always motivated by a desire to seize power. God had given Adam dominion and control over the earth which conveyed a sense of entitlement and ownership. Defeating him would provide the spoils of war and give Satan a place where he could set up his own kingdom and exercise power over man. Since God's authority and rulership were clearly established in the heavens, Satan's plan was to establish his power and authority in the earth and Adam stood in his way.

Fear:

Satan would have been concerned about God's intent in creating Adam. Was God in some way grooming Adam to be a warrior who would challenge him? A righteous Adam posed a clear and present danger to him since Adam could, if he developed spiritual authority, eventually rise up and challenge Satan. While Satan was not afraid of who Adam was at that time, he was concerned about what he might become in the future. Adam therefore became the prime target of God's enemy and Satan's guns were now aimed at him.

Strategic evaluation:
From what we have seen so far, it appears that Satan's agenda was aggressive, driven by dark motives and in some cases predictable. From the very day Adam was created, it

was inevitable that Satan would go after him to destroy him. In contrast, God's agenda so far has *not* been easy to follow. Why did He create man? Why give him dominion in the earth? Didn't He realize that this would make Adam a target for Satan? Did He miscalculate the risks? It seems that, if God *does* have a plan, it is not working out well at all. Either that, or He is not yet ready to reveal His true strategic agenda and is keeping it hidden beneath the surface.

> All these things Jesus spoke to the multitude in parables; and without a parable He did not speak to them, that it might be fulfilled which was spoken by the prophet, saying, "I will open my mouth in parables; I will utter things kept secret from the foundation of the world".
> (Matthew 13:34-35)

Rest assured that God never miscalculates. His plan was in effect even before the beginning, but it was deliberately "kept secret from the foundation of the world", so that His enemy would not be able to anticipate His true intentions, until the very end. However, God did provide insights into His strategic agenda hidden in Scripture, as we will discover with increasing clarity as we continue our investigation.

That is the nature of a perfect strategy. Effective strategy is not just knowing what to do, but executing your plan in such a way that your opponent does not recognize your true intent, until it is too late. This is the approach that God takes to destroy the works of the evil one.

The nature of the battle has now changed. Satan is no longer limited to challenging God or His angels directly. He has found another, much easier target in man and plans to use this creature whom God loves, as a dispensable tool in his guerrilla warfare against God.

We next go to the Garden of Eden, to witness the inevitable showdown between Satan and the unsuspecting Adam.

CHAPTER 4

THE BATTLE OF EDEN

The contest between Satan and Adam in the Garden provides the background for how these two beings became eternal enemies. Eden connects us to our spiritual ancestry and is really the starting point of the history of man's existence on the earth. It provides insights into who we are, why we behave the way we do, and what God plans for us in the future.

Satan launched a brutal, unprovoked attack on Adam in the Garden because he sensed that Adam had an important, even vital role to play in God's strategic plan. Exactly what that role would be was not exactly clear to Satan. However, he knew that he had to act quickly to neutralize Adam before God could use him effectively. So, what was God's plan for Adam, and by extension, for us his spiritual descendants? What role do we play in God's strategic plan?

To see the whol
unrelated events
thousands of year:
same strategic th
happened in Eden, l
these two pivotal ever

Event 1: Man is appo.
"Master of all he survey

In Genesis, God gives
commissions:

> Then God blessed them, a.   .u said unto them, "Be
> fruitful and multiply; fill the earth, and subdue it; have
> dominion over the fish of the sea and over the birds of the
> air and over everything that moves on the earth."
> (Genesis 1:28)

This directive places man at the top of the food chain and
gives him authority to:

1. Multiply in number and fill the earth.

2. Subdue all living things and have dominion over
   them.

God commissioned man to be the *dominant species* in the
natural world, subduing all the creatures of the earth and
bringing them under his mastery. Looking back over time,
we can see that we have successfully carried out this
assignment. Man has multiplied to fill every corner of the
world, and for the most part, our lives are sustained either
by the animals we have tamed and now breed for food, or
the wilderness we conquered and converted to farmlands.

ntinues to exercise dominion by
to exploit every natural resource in
ablish systems of government and
acilitate orderly rule. So, yes, man has
n carrying out the first great commission. But
s also a second great commission, which, like the
st, instructed man to exercise authority and dominion in
the earth:

**Event 2: Man is appointed to a position of spiritual
authority in the Earth.**

> And He said unto them, "Go ye into all the world and
> preach the gospel to every creature. He who believes and is
> baptized will be saved; but he who does not believe will be
> condemned. And these signs will follow those who believe:
> In my name they shall cast out demons; they will speak with
> new tongues; they shall take up serpents; and if they drink
> anything deadly, it will by no means hurt them; they will lay
> hands on the sick, and they will recover."
> (Mark 16:15-18)

This second directive given by Jesus before His ascension
to heaven, is very similar to the first except that here, the
intent and application is *spiritual*. Jesus authorized and
empowered His disciples to:

1. Go into all the earth.

2. Bring every "creature" under the influence of the
    gospel.

3. Exercise dominion over demons, serpents (spiritual
    reference to Satan and his horde) and sickness.

These two "great commissions" given to man by the same Person, the Word, at an interval of time spanning many thousands of years, *are really connecting parts of the same strategic thought.* Here are the parallels between what God said to Adam, and then to His disciples later on:

- God's first commission shows an intention to establish man as the dominant species in the natural world. His second commission, demonstrates His plan to establish man as the dominant spiritual authority on the earth.

- The first commission was meant for a natural man, created out of the dust of the earth. His assignment was a physical task. The second commission was given to a spiritual man or a new creation, born not of flesh but of the Spirit of God. (John 3:6). His spiritual assignment is to play a role in ensuring that God's strategic will "be done on earth as it is in heaven" (Matt:6:10).

- In each commission, God *specifically* identifies man's targets for him. In the first, man's assigned targets are natural creatures, the beasts of the field, the birds of the air, the fish of the sea. In the second commission, the targets identified for man are evil spiritual beings, demons and "serpents" and destructive spiritual conditions such as sickness and damnation.

- God gave man specific tools to accomplish each commission. The natural man was created with a strong body and a keen mind to enable him to physically subdue the earth. The power tool given to the spiritual man to transform the earth is the preaching of the gospel. The Apostle Paul who dedicated his life to this mission had this to say:

> For I am not ashamed of the gospel of Christ, for it is the power of God to salvation for everyone who believes; for the Jew first and also for the Greek. (Romans 1:16)

The gospel is the power that God placed in man's hand to exercise spiritual authority, and in order for God's will to be done on earth as it is in heaven, the preaching of the gospel has to become a priority for all spiritual men and women.

- Both commissions require man to develop progressive abilities. In the natural order of things, the physical man has to mature from childhood to adulthood, develop muscles, acquire useful skills, and learn the process of exercising physical authority. So too must the spiritual man grow up from new-born babe, to the point of spiritual maturity. To be effective for God, we must all become accustomed to walking in the spirit, putting on the whole armor of God, and wielding the sword of the spirit to accomplish His purposes in the earth. This is why the Apostle Peter encourages us:

> As new born babes desire the pure milk of the word that you may grow thereby.
> (1 Peter 2:2)

God expects that we will grow in grace and in the knowledge of the Lord Jesus, to become spiritual men and women, capable of exercising Godly authority in the earth.

At this point the picture is becoming clearer. God's plan for man was and is for him to dominate the earth both physically and spiritually. God's strategic intent was to establish man as both the physical *and* spiritual authority, first in the Garden of Eden and later in the world. I believe that the Garden was God's training ground for Adam, to teach him how to exercise dominion in a controlled environment before releasing him to dominate the rest of the earth, since that was where his ultimate responsibility and destiny lay.

However, what God meant as a place of blessing and training for Adam, Satan intended to convert by perversion, to a place of bondage, distress and a curse over Adam's life. This is the enemy's constant war against us; to try to take the very thing that God intends as a blessing in our lives and use it against us. The Apostle Peter cautions us all:

> Be sober, be vigilant because your adversary the devil, walks about like a roaring lion, seeking whom he may devour.
> (1Peter: 5:8)

God has given each and every one of us something of value, *a garden of our own*, to manage on His behalf. That garden may be in the form of a talent we possess, "natural" ability we have, or thing of value we have acquired. For some, it is a musical gift (like Lucifer had) or the ability to form creative ideas, win people over, or wealth we earn or inherit. One particular area of interest for me is in helping Christian business owners to maximize the financial and spiritual potential of their businesses.

It is important that we do not take God's blessing for granted, but to recognize that like Adam, *we are stewards of His favor* and ultimately accountable to Him for what we do with what He entrusts to us.

Satan's new plan *was to convert the Garden into a battlefield* and although he is not all knowing, and probably did not understand God's full purpose for Adam, he is cunning enough to realize that Adam's presence there was not in his own best interests. Having connected God's complete commission to man, we now return to the battle between Satan, and God's man in the Earth, Adam, in Genesis chapter 2.

> Then the Lord God took the man and put him into the garden of Eden to tend and keep it. And the Lord God commanded the man saying, "Of every tree of the garden you may freely eat; but out of the tree of the knowledge of good and evil you shall not eat, for in the day that you eat of it you shall surely die".
> (Genesis: 2:15-17)

In this passage of Scripture, we find the very first commandment that God gave to man: "you shall not eat of it (the fruit)". This commandment carried a warning of dire consequence for disobedience, "for in the day that you eat of it you shall surely die". God could not have said this any clearer to Adam. The day you eat this fruit, *you will die!*

As part of his due diligence on Adam, Satan would have made note of this very important instruction, because of the severity of consequence it carried. Adam was the first man who ever lived, which meant that no one had seen a man die before, so it would have been unclear to Satan what would occur if Adam actually ate the fruit. Would he instantly collapse and fall to the ground? Would he crumble back into the dust from which he was created? I don't think that any of the angels or demons in the audience, really knew what to expect, except that according to God's word to Adam, the "wages of sin" (Romans 6:23) would be *death*.

It appears that when God gave Adam this instruction, Eve was not around to hear it because according to the timing of the events related in scripture, she was not yet created. Although Adam no doubt would have repeated God's instruction to her, this was to some extent second hand information and Eve may or may not have grasped the severity of it all. This presented a great opportunity for Satan to implement his plan. Scripture does not tell us whether Satan tried and failed to convince Adam to eat the fruit before he approached Eve. It does tell us however, that he was successful in his efforts to tempt her to do so.

> Now the serpent was more cunning than any beast of the field which the Lord God had made. And he said unto the woman, "Has God indeed said, "You shall not eat of every tree of the garden?" And the woman said unto the serpent, "We may eat of the fruit of the trees of the garden; but of the fruit of the tree which is in the midst of the garden, God has said, "You shall not eat of it, nor shall ye touch it lest you die". Then the serpent said to the woman, "Ye shall not surely die".
> (Genesis 3:1-4)

As human beings, Adam and Eve could not see into the spirit realm. They recognized God by the sound of His voice as He "walked in the garden in the cool of the day" (Genesis 3:8). Satan realized that as a spirit, he would be limited in his ability to appeal to Eve's natural appetites and tempt her to eat the fruit. As a result, he took on the form of a physical being to manipulate her through her physical senses. (Interesting parallel, Satan took on the form of a physical being to entice and enslave Eve, God took on the form of a physical being to save man.)

Satan chose the serpent to deliver his message because it was the most crafty, sly creature in the garden.

Remember the point we made in chapter one about hostile corporate takeovers? They are "usually the work of a cunning mastermind, developing and implementing strategic moves in secret, catching everyone, including the intended victim, completely unawares." We now introduce the first and ultimate hostile takeover, planned and executed by an evil genius, where the intended victim is Adam, and the asset targeted, is control over the entire earth.

The serpent told Eve two things:

1. God is lying to you, you will not die.

2. God is holding out on you. He doesn't want you to eat the fruit because he doesn't want you to become wise (Genesis 2:5).

Using a combination of blatant lies and half-truths, Satan persuaded Eve to disobey God, and she in turn persuaded Adam to do the same. By their actions they were saying in essence: "God, we don't believe you. We believe this here snake, and appoint him the authority over our lives. Your word cannot be trusted, and we make the choice to live our lives based on what the snake tells us from now on."

These are the same age-old, tested and proven weapons Satan uses on man today. His first trick is to try to convince us, as he did with Eve, that God's word is irrelevant and of no consequence to our lives and decisions. Rather than ask us what God did, or did not say ("Has God indeed said?"), he dispenses with God's word altogether and tells us that we can figure things out for ourselves.

His new approach is to get us to believe that our thinking has "evolved" to a higher level than that of our ancestors and as a result, modern human reasoning becomes the replacement for eternal truth. It seems that the more "enlightened" man has become, the more he relies on himself and the less he believes in God. The truth is that despite man's growing intellect, God's word is still applicable as the final authority, and believing Satan's lie places man in the same eternal danger in which Eve unfortunately found herself.

The second deception that Satan uses against man is to convince us that God does not have our best interests at heart. Satan sometimes uses circumstances in our lives to present God as deliberately holding back and depriving us of the things that we *think* we need or deserve from him.

When we find ourselves asking questions like:

- "Why me God?" or

- "What have I done to deserve this, Lord?" or

- "Where were you when this was happening to me, Lord?"

we are showing signs that we have begun to doubt God's loving intention toward us and to mistrust the assurances of His word concerning us. Ultimately Satan's intention here is to drive a wedge into our relationship with God and make us unable to trust that God knows best, and is "working all things together for our good" (Romans 8:28). While Satan has adapted his tactics to change with the times, his underlying plan of attack on man is still to use doubt and deceit *to produce disobedience*. So what happened to Adam and Eve after they disobeyed God and ate the fruit? Physically, they lived for many more years. But spiritually, they were cut off from God and exiled from the garden on that very day. Adam's disobedience introduced a new condition to the human race, *sin.*

Genesis 2: 7 tells us that when God created man and breathed into his nostrils the breath of life, man became a "living being." When man disobeyed God that part of him, his spirit, which enabled him to have a relationship with God (Who is a Spirit), died. Not only did Adam die spiritually because of his sin, but he lost his God-given authority to be a spiritual influence on the earth. As we saw, this was Satan's strategic intent all along, to neutralize Adam as a potential threat. Adam and his descendants were now all spiritually dead, and as long as they continued in this state they would pose no danger to Satan.

It is clear that Satan scored a significant victory in getting man to disobey God. In one strategic move, he deposed Adam as God's appointed authority, and replaced him as the dominant spiritual influence on the earth. God gave dominion to Adam and Adam relinquished it to Satan. Legally therefore, Satan became the supreme ruler with the right to exercise dominion over man. This is why in 2 Corinthians 4:4 Paul refers to Satan as "the god of this age" and in John 14: 30 Jesus Himself referred to Satan as the "ruler of this world".

God must have been grieved by Adam's sin. When He confronted Eve about her disobedience, He asked the question:

"What is this that you have done?"
(Genesis 3:13

The tone of the question is much the same as that of a human parent confronting a child who committed an appalling offense. It is one of incredulous disbelief that the child could do something so stupid. Although God was not taken by surprise, I believe He was grieved by Adam's sin and the thought of the judgment to come. God has a father's heart and feels deep grief at our sin, because sin carries the consequence of death. In Ephesians 4:30, Paul's plead to us is "do not grieve the Holy Spirit" by harboring sin in our lives.

In addition to neutralizing Adam as a potential threat, Satan may have had another objective in view. You may remember I suggested previously, that one of Satan's original objectives was to try to have God impeached so he could lay claim to a vacant Throne. As we shall see in chapter seven, ("Enter the dragon's lair"), Satan attempted to trap Jesus in the wilderness in this manner, and I believe that he may have been trying to do the same with God in Eden. That outcome would depend on God's response to Adam's sin.

As human parents we act instinctively to protect our children from harm or hurt. This instinct is so strong that parents have been known to break laws, or conceal an illegal act, to shield a child from consequences. So, what if in a moment of grief, God decided, "I am sovereign, and therefore I pardon you, Adam, for this sin,". Not an uncommon thing for a human parent to do. Had God done this, He would have broken His own word, declaring the laws of heaven invalid by using His power for unjust means. That would have made him legally unfit to sit on the Throne, which is why I believe Satan was hoping that God would yield to this moral dilemma, and act in a way that would invalidate His divine right to rule.

Despite His love for Adam, God could not spare him from judgment, or find some loophole to excuse his sin, in the same way that He could not spare Jesus later on, when He volunteered to take upon Himself the sin of the world. In Romans 8:23 Paul said "He who did not spare His own son, but delivered Him for us all" referring to Jesus' judgment as the Lamb of God on our behalf. This speaks to God's divine character. As much as He loves us, there must be accountability and consequence for sin.

At that point, God's strategic dilemma was finding an appropriate response to the damage done in Eden. How does God reach out in love to Adam and to us and, at the same time, uphold the truth and justice of His Word?

For God *so* loved the world:

Human parental love is sacrificial love and many parents would give everything they have, including surrendering their own lives, to save that of an offspring. In my opinion, this parental instinct of "take me instead", separates man from all other living creatures. In this regard, the Stanford University Metaphysics Research Lab, makes a distinction between "biological altruism" and true altruism. According to Stanford researchers, truly altruistic behavior requires "conscious intent of helping another." Animals display biological altruism (instinctively defend their young) but lack the "conscious intent" to display true altruism. Only man has this capacity.

In other words, while some animals will instinctively risk their lives to defend their young, when their efforts are proving futile, *none* will step forward and say to the predator, "my life for that of my offspring; take me instead". Rather than be eaten by the predator, the survival instinct takes over and every animal would at the very last minute, run away and live to reproduce another day. Not so with us. Human beings have the ability to override our survival instinct, *make a conscious decision,* and say: "take me instead". This ability to willingly surrender our life for the sake of those we love, is unique to God, and to man who was created in His image and likeness.

Sacrificial love now provides the basis of God's response to man's eternal problem caused by sin. God's love for man is so potent, that He decides to take the consequence of sin upon Himself and pay the ultimate price on our behalf. Jesus in explaining His motivation to go to the cross said this:

> "Greater love has no one than this, than to lay down one's life for his friends."
> (John 15:13)

I believe that God placed this ability in us so that we could relate to the powerful emotion that literally compelled Jesus to go to the cross. **Jesus' response to the righteous judgment of God was, "take Me instead".** While this is a position taken purely out of love, it also serves a higher, strategic purpose in the plan of God, as we shall see later on.

So, for those of us keeping track of the score, it would seem that Satan registered a major victory in the Garden of Eden. We have to wonder at this point whether God's plan was completely derailed by man's disobedience, or whether this was part of something far more significant that He was working on.

Satan and man are now eternal enemies and as Adam and Eve leave the garden to carry out the first commission of multiplying and subduing the earth, the hidden war taking place in the spiritual realm follow them and their descendants wherever they go. While Satan's hatred for all men is obvious, the focus of the battle now moves away from two people, to a group of people, or a nation that God describes this way:

> For you are a holy people to the Lord your God; the Lord your God has chosen you to be a people for Himself, a special treasure above all the peoples on the face of the earth.
> (Deuteronomy 7:6)

CHAPTER 5

GOD'S CHOSEN PEOPLE

In this chapter we will examine what happened to the human race after Adam and Eve were ejected from Eden, how God was able to establish a strategic foothold in earth via a chosen people and the significance of this people to His long term plan for man. After Adam disobeyed God and was expelled from Eden, sin, and death by sin, became a feature of every man's life. God had commissioned Adam to be fruitful, to multiply and replenish the earth. This instruction however, was given to a sinless man who had not yet entered the Garden of Eden.

When Adam sinned and broke off fellowship with God, the original commission to replenish the earth could not be revoked, since God could not go back on His word. As a result, as fallen man multiplied, the effects of sin spread throughout the earth like a plague.

Genesis 6 tells us that by the time of Noah, the world of men was divided into two camps:

1. Godly men: there were a very few, actually, just Noah and his family, who had heard of the creator

God and wanted to have fellowship with Him (Genesis 6:8 *"Noah found grace in the eyes of the Lord"*) and

2. All others on earth, who felt that they were their own god and wanted nothing to do with the God of heaven.

Satan's strategy in dealing with the human race was (and still is today) to keep man blind to his existence and to the war that he was waging in our midst. The events of Eden had established Satan as the "god of this age" and man, his spiritual property, to be manipulated and controlled as he saw fit. Having secured the fall of man by disobedience, Satan followed him throughout the earth inciting him in open rebellion against God.

> Then the Lord saw that the wickedness of man was great in the earth, and that every intent of the thoughts of his heart was only evil continually. And the Lord was sorry that He had made man on the earth and He was grieved in His heart. (Genesis 6:5-6)

In this passage of Scripture we see a side of God that reveals much about His character. **Sin causes God to grieve**. Grief flows out of a broken heart and can be a much stronger emotion than anger. Children sometimes do things which anger their parents. If you gave your child some instruction and he/she failed to carry it out, you may become annoyed, upset and even angry. There are times however when the infraction is so serious and the consequence so severe, that it causes the parent to grieve. Grief of this nature comes out of concern for consequences.

While I don't wish this on any parent, if for example a child commits a serious crime and is arrested, the parent's reaction quickly grows from a feeling of anger at what the child had done, to heart break and grief over the consequences to follow.

In the same way, God the Father, wasn't just angry at man's sin, *He was grieved* because of the consequences that He knew would follow. The people of Noah's day had become so rebellious and sinful that God could no longer hold back judgment. That judgment came via a flood that destroyed all life on the earth except those preserved in the ark that Noah built. As soon as the flood had subsided and the earth was repopulated, man's sin nature drove him right back to where he was before the flood, *enmity with God.*

Satan would have counted the flood as yet another major victory. It would seem that, because of man's fallen nature, he was destined to live under God's constant judgment and there was very little God could do about this. However, God still had an eternal purpose for man, but man clearly could not fulfill that divine destiny in a sin infected state. Finding a way to save man from sin now became an important consideration in God's strategic plan.

To do this, God would need to establish a toe hold in a world that was now hostile to, and alienated from Him. What God needed was an ally on earth, a man who could sense God's presence in his life and would be willing to walk before Him in obedience. Abram of Ur of the Chaldees, was such a man. God saw in Abram the qualities He was looking for as a basis for establishing a relationship with man.

Now the Lord had said to Abram, "Get thee out of your country, from your family and from your father's house, to a land that I will show you. I will make you a great nation; I

will bless you and make your name great; and you will be a blessing. I will bless those who bless you and curse him who curses you and in you shall all families of the earth be blessed".
(Genesis 12:1-3)

It is interesting that God required Abram to leave the comfort and security of his father's house, cut ties with his family, leave his country and go on a journey to some unknown place that God will show him.

Many of us would have said, "Lord, tell me where you are taking me *first* and then I'll tell you if I will go". How many of us would respond positively to the following instruction: "Son/daughter, say goodbye to your friends and family, pack your bags, take your family to the airport. When you get there, I'll tell you where you're going and *then* you can buy your ticket".

In those days, travel to distant lands was always potentially dangerous. There were no international protocols on safe passage, no passports to facilitate border crossings and of course there was always the risk that someone could attack and rob you, or in Abram's case, take your wife from you by force.

Abram had to completely trust God and put his life and the lives of his family in His hands. It's easy for us to trust God when things are going great in our lives, but when major challenges emerge and there is no safe harbor in sight, staying calm and trusting God takes faith, a lot of faith. That is where Abram (later renamed Abraham by God) through his faith in God, established himself as an anchor for the soul of all men. He was the first human who learned to walk by faith and willingly put his life in the hands of God unconditionally.

Abram's act of obedience was in a way, different from Noah's earlier on. God had convinced Noah that the flood was coming and he knew that he would die if he did not get on board that ark. Yes, it took faith to build the ark when there wasn't a cloud in sight, but Noah was in a sense, responding to an urgent situation and *had* to trust God. In contrast, Abram was not in any immediate peril when God called him. In fact, he had every reason to ignore God and stay right where he was. He came from a wealthy family, had a good job, a safe and comfortable home, nice 401K, attractive sixty-five year old wife. So why leave? Abram left Haran because God instructed him to. Abram's response was an act of obedience based on simple faith in God.

This is exactly the type of relationship God wanted to establish with Adam earlier on. The root of Adam's sin was not open rebellion, but a lack of simple faith in God. Compare Adam's action to that of the prodigal son of Luke 15:11. The prodigal son *demanded* his inheritance and left his father's home to go live a life of excess, in absolute defiance of his father's wishes and intentions for him. That is open rebellion.

Adam's sin was foolishly allowing himself to be influenced by his wife to eat the fruit, knowing full well that it was wrong to do so. It was not being committed enough to trust God and do what was right, by rejecting his wife's persuasive appeals. Adam probably could not bear the thought of separation from Eve and therefore chose to eat the fruit to show solidarity with her. The lesson here is that while we may not be living in open rebellion to God, our lack of faith to take a stand and do what He expects of us, is just as harmful.

God asked Abraham to put Him before family twice, first to leave his home and then later to sacrifice his son. Abraham never hesitated or doubted his hearing of God's voice in either case. At last, God had found the faith needed to establish a covenant with man. This was the strategic toe-hold He was looking for. Genesis 22: 1-18 tells us that one day God made a very unusual, even humanly absurd request of Abraham. God told him to take his only son Isaac, go up into the mountains and sacrifice him on an altar. The normal human reaction to this would be "this can't be God speaking to me". Abraham however had walked closely with God for a very long time and knew His voice. This *was* God and He was serious about this request.

Abraham did not hesitate. He took *his only begotten son,* Issac, went to the mountain, placed him on an altar and raised his knife to take his life. As he was about to plunge the knife into Issac's chest, the Angel of the Lord shouted from heaven *"Abraham, Abraham!"* and stopped him in his tracks.

> And He said, "Do not lay your hand on the lad, or do anything to him; for I know that you fear God, since you have not withheld your son, your only son, from Me." (Genesis 22:12)

Whew! That was close. Abraham passed God's test with flying colors. But this was not really about Abraham neither was it just a random test of his faith. God was engineering something very significant, very strategic in this unusual situation. He was establishing the basis for a binding contract that would ultimately save mankind.

God had to find a solution to the problem of sin on His own, since all men were sinners and could do nothing to help themselves. To do this He needed a *legal basis* on which to intervene in man's affairs. Satan had established his legal right to destroy the human race by getting Adam to disobey God and switch allegiance to him.

For God to intervene now, He too needed a legal basis to do so. Had He just sent Jesus to die for our sins,

Satan would have cried foul. "What gives *You* the right to interfere in man's affairs and send a savior? Man is under my dominion!" Just as Adam's disobedience gave Satan the legal right to enslave man, Abraham's obedience provided God with the legal right to intervene and deliver us. This contractual right was established in the same way that binding agreements are made on the earth.

Lets say that you hire me to paint your house. Our contract is based on the exchange of something of value (or "consideration"). The deal is, I paint your house and you pay me the price we agreed upon. In the case of the agreement between God and Abraham, the thing of value exchanged was the lives of their respective "only sons". Anything less would not have been appropriate. The basis of this spiritual agreement is "you sacrifice your son for me (or at least be willing to do so) and I will send my Son to die as a sacrifice for you (and the entire human race)".

Abraham did not understand any of this at the time, nor was he aware of the eternal importance of what God was doing; he was just acting in obedience. To God, this was a critical part of His strategic plan and He formalized it with a profound, divine declaration:

> "By Myself I have sworn says the Lord, because you have done this thing, and have not withheld your son, your only son- blessing I will bless you, and multiplying I will multiply your descendants as the stars of the heaven and as the sand which is on the seashore; and your descendants shall possess the gate of their enemies. In your seed all the nations of the earth shall be blessed because you have obeyed My voice".
> (Genesis 22:17-18)

Because of Abraham's willingness to actually sacrifice his son ("done this thing") God swore by the highest authority there is, *Himself*, that He would send the messiah, who would be one of Abraham's descendants, ("in *your seed all the nations of the earth* will be blessed") to redeem man. God had now established an iron clad agreement with man to send a savior **and no devil in hell could challenge that.** Today we recognize Abraham as not just the father of a physical nation Israel, but as father of a spiritual nation, a people living in a Kingdom without physical borders and who, like Abraham have a relationship with God that is based on faith.

We said earlier on that God often uses the physical to foreshadow the spiritual. As we will see next, God used the physical nation of Israel the direct descendants of Abraham, as the vehicle through which a spiritual nation the Church would later be born. Abraham's spiritual descendants throughout the world are indeed as numerous as the stars in the heavens.

God announces His chosen people Israel to the world:

If Abraham was God's initial toe-hold in a sinful world, Israel would be His strategic foot-hold later on. After Abraham died, God established a tribe from his descendants, called the descendants of Israel, or "children of Israel". Israel formerly known as Jacob, was Abraham's grandson.

> When the Most High divided their inheritance to the nations, when He separated the sons of Adam, He set the boundaries of the peoples according to the number of the children of Israel. For the Lord's portion is His people; Jacob is the place of His inheritance.
> (Deuteronomy 32:8-9)

Again, referring to the children of Israel, God said:

> "For you are a holy people unto the Lord your God; the

Lord thy God has chosen you to be a people for Himself, a special treasure above all people on the face of the earth" (Deuteronomy 7:6)

God identifies the nation of Israel by use of the following terms: "holy people unto the Lord", "chosen", "special", "above all people on the face of the earth". Why did God do this? Why select a specific group of people, out of all the inhabitants of the earth, as His chosen people? Well, it certainly wasn't because they loved Him, or wanted Him to be their God. God often referred to them in scripture as a "stiff-necked" rebellious people, who rejected His ways. *So what was their strategic value to God?*

God chose Israel because they were the fulfillment of His promise to Abraham.

God had made a special promise to Abraham. "Because you obeyed Me, I will make a great nation out of your descendants." Notice that God did not make the promise to Abraham so that he *would* obey. Sometimes we may say to our child, if you get a good report card you will get this reward. Abraham, obeyed first, *then* got the promise of the blessing, and being therefore justified by faith, proved himself worthy of the inheritance that God promised him.

God established Israel as a great nation, because of His unbreakable promise to Abraham. Though Abraham died long before the nation of Israel was born, God kept His word and delivered on His promise. The nation of Israel is a testament of God's faithfulness to Abraham and by extension to all of us. It provides a blessed assurance, that even though our time on earth may expire, God will keep His eternal promise to us, as He did to Abraham.

God chose Israel to demonstrate His presence and power to the world.

Satan employs two strategies against man:

- Try to convince us that he does not exist and, failing that

- Try to convince us, as he did with Eve, that he does not mean us any harm, but rather is on our side against a restrictive God.

His strategy is an effective one, since, the more we understand how much he really hates us and wants to destroy us, the more likely we will be to take God seriously. Many people come to God through the preaching of the gospel, which explains that there is eternal judgment for sin. Satan's ploy is to keep his existence and the reality of judgment the biggest secret in the world. His plan for man depends on keeping us in darkness and ignorance.

On the other hand, God's plan has always been to bring man into the light. He wants us to understand that He is real, His love is real and that eternity is real. So, how does an invisible God go about persuading the world that He is very real? In John 3:8, Jesus told Nicodemus that while we can't see the wind, we know that it is real because of its effect in the natural world. In the same way, God needed an identifiable group of people, a nation, to act as a wind gauge, so the rest of us could recognize the effects of His intervention in their lives and history and know that He is real.

Probably the most memorable example of this, was God's intervention to deliver Israel from slavery in Egypt. Genesis chapter 50 tells us that after Joseph (Abraham's great-grandson) passed away, the children of Israel established a home for themselves in the land of Egypt in a place called Goshen. Usually when a small group of people settle in a larger nation, they are eventually assimilated into the new society. Not so with these clannish Israelites. Instead of them embracing Egyptian culture and society, they keep to themselves and begin multiplying faster than rabbits. Pretty soon they become a potential threat to Egypt's national security. No nation would allow another nation, which refuses to bend to its ways, to expand within its secured borders. Pharaoh decides, in the interest of national security, to enslave the Israelites and keep them under the control of the military.

After years of them crying out under the whip, God sends a man Moses, to tell mighty Pharaoh to let His people go. God was about to introduce Himself to the nations of the world in an unmistakable and dramatic way. Egypt was a powerful nation and here we have this son of a slave, Moses, attempting to dictate terms to their commander in chief. Pharaoh did not know this God that Moses represented, but he was about to find out who He was, *the hard way.* God had told Abraham that He would deal harshly with (that is "curse") anyone who opposed Israel. He revealed Himself to Pharaoh and to the world as the God who would defend His people against all enemies, *natural and spiritual.*

As God obliterated the armies of Egypt and led Israel out of slavery, Moses and his people were feared and respected wherever they went. The world now knew that the invisible God of Heaven was their God and He would fight for them throughout the ages. In this scenario, God used Israel to prove to Egypt and the world at large, that He is real and His word is not to be trifled with.

God chose the Israelites to define sin to the world.

God is holy and sin will be judged. *But does man know what sin is?* How could God hold man accountable for sin, unless He provides some definition of what it is? God told Adam that if he ate the fruit, he would die. Adam knew what the law was for him. If God did not speak this to Adam, there would be no law and there would be no sin if he ate. But what about the rest of us? How would we know what sin is?

God chose the Israelites to be the recipients and custodians of His law, which would expressly state what He means by sin. Sin is breaking the law of God. God has provided man, via decrees given to Israel, details of His law, so that if we break any of these in letter or spirit, we are guilty of sin and therefore deserving of judgment.

> Because the law brings about wrath; for where there is no law, there is no transgression.
> (Romans 4:15)

Now, if we take the time to go through that entire list, we very soon realize that we have all at some time or another, broken God's law and are therefore sinners. Man's issue is no longer how to recognize sin, *but what to do about it.* There are a number of options for us to consider.

1. We can imitate Adam, hide and hope that God will not find us out. That did not work out well for him, and it will not work for us. Surprisingly, this is the option taken by many people today. We think that because something is done under cover of darkness that no-one sees. Well, maybe no human will see, but our every sin, both public and private, is on our

spiritual record. In Numbers 32:23, God warns *"be sure your sin will find you out"*. There is no hiding from the consequences of sin.

2. We can attempt to excuse ourselves or justify the sin as serving a higher good. We are probably all aware of instances where people justify dishonesty in small doses because it provides a greater benefit, usually financial. There are no small lies, white lies or innocent lies. It is instinctive in fallen man, to try to justify or evade responsibility for personal sin. "The serpent beguiled me". "The woman *you* gave me, she made me do it". "I came from a broken home". "It was a moment of weakness". All very persuasive arguments in themselves, however none of these work as an antidote or as atonement for sin.

3. We could ignore God and His laws altogether and maybe He will go away. Sometimes people ignore their issues, hoping that they eventually sort themselves out. Maybe some do, but not this one. Like Adam we will all have to face God one day and answer for our sin. The question is, *do you have a good lawyer?* The Apostle John told us where we can get the very best in legal representation:

My little children, these things I write to you, so that you may not sin. And if anyone sins, we have an Advocate with the Father, Jesus Christ the righteous.
(1John 2:1)

God chose Israel to provide the solution for sin to the world:

It seems that regardless of which direction we turn, sin has laid a trap for us. We all have constructive notice of sin in our lives, because God gave His law to man through Israel. Now this ordinarily would be a hopeless situation, since man seems to have no way out. But in the same way that God is just, He is also merciful and forgiving and has also, through the Israelites, provided a way for us to avoid the consequences of sin. God provided the following formula to deal with sin:

> And according to the law almost all things are purified with blood, without the shedding of blood there is no remission. (Hebrews 9:22)

Without the shedding of blood there is no remission or forgiveness for sin. The only way that sin could be atoned for is that something or *someone* innocent has to die. The basis of this principle is that the *wages of sin is death*. Sin has the unavoidable consequence of death. So it is either you die, or someone else dies in your place. To drive home this point to us, God had the Israelites sacrifice prized animals every year to temporarily atone for their sin. This practice started in Eden when God killed animals to provide physical and spiritual covering for Adam's sin, it was repeated in Egypt when God had the Israelites kill a lamb and sprinkle its blood over their doors and it ended from God's perspective, when Jesus was crucified on the cross. God was, through the nation of Israel showing man both the nature of his problem and the solution that was to come.

God used the nation of Israel to show His character and nature to His spiritual people, the Church:

We now introduce the Church, God's redeemed, chosen spiritual people and the ultimate focal point of His entire strategic plan. We will examine this group later on, to determine who they are and their purpose in God's plan. But for now, what we need to understand is that the church, which came into existence after Jesus' resurrection, needs a point of reference to past events which shape its present relationship with God.

God was, in His documented dealings with Israel, revealing to the church aspects of His divine character and the details of His plan to free us from sin. If we did not have the history of Israel as recorded in Scripture, we would not understand God's eternal plan for man. The entire foundation of the gospels, all of the teachings of the Lord Jesus, as well as the letters written by the apostles explaining salvation, point back to the Old Testament. The record of God's dealing with Israel as documented in scripture provides us with living examples of how to function today as the people of God. *Their natural history is our spiritual history.*

This is what I believe God was referring to when He told Abraham that his descendants will be like the stars in the heavens and the sands of the sea. Included in the headcount of Abraham's physical and spiritual descendants are all the Jewish people who ever lived, as well as Gentiles who put their faith in God's plan of salvation from the time of Jesus' resurrection to the day of His eventual return. Get all these people together in one place and they would appear to be a multitude that is almost impossible to count, just as the sand of the sea.

God chose the Israelites as a strategic weapon in His battle with Satan.

I believe that Satan monitors everything that God says to and about man for clues as to God's strategic agenda. Satan has in many instances used scripture references to suit his needs. In speaking to Eve, he knew what God said to her about eating from the tree and he quoted scripture references from the book of Psalms in his contest with Jesus in the wilderness.

God's promise to Abraham that he would make of him a great nation would not have escaped Satan's attention. As soon as God identified Israel as His chosen people, they became a target for Satan. Satan hated Israel because they were the people created out of a promise made by God. His plan, down through the ages, has been to cause other nations to rise up against the Jews, kill as many of them as they could and at times even incite Israel to rebel against God, so that God's judgment would befall them.

A friend of mine who is a devout Muslim, once said to me that modern Israel is a pampered privileged nation that always gets things their way and have the major military powers of the world bowing to them. There have always been military advantages to Israel being the people of God. Down through the ages, Israel has constantly been at war with surrounding nations, as it sought to carve out its homeland in territories already occupied by other people. In many of these wars, the Lord has fought for them and gave them victory.

For example we have:
Numbers 2: 1-3, battle with the Canaanites

Numbers 21: 21-35, battle with the Amorites

Numbers 31: 1-8, battle with the Midianites

Joshua 6:1-25, battle of Jericho

Joshua 10:1-13, battle with the Amorite Kings

In each of these battles, as well as in many others, God's direct intervention secured major victories for Israel, against great odds. The fact that the tiny nation of Israel wields unexplainable military power and influence today should surprise no-one. But while there have been great military benefits to being God's chosen people, there have also been severe consequences. Satan has been intent on destroying Israel as a nation from its very inception. For example, one of the methods of population control imposed by Pharaoh back in Moses' day, was to kill all the male Jewish children as soon as they were born. Killing male Jewish babies has always been a tactic of Satan because he knew that one day, according to what the prophets were saying, one such child would rise up and lead God's people in battle against him. The practice of killing Jewish babies occurred immediately before the birth of Moses and then later, before Jesus was born.

The nation of Israel has been under attack since the time of its formation and while it has won many victories, it has also suffered heavy casualties. The Jews have been enslaved and despised wherever in the world they went. According to the Jewish Virtual Library, by 1933 there were about nine and a half million Jews living in Europe. By the time the Nazis took over Europe in 1943, six million, or two out of every three Jews, had been targeted and slaughtered.

Even today, there is a strong sentiment against Israel

and its occupation of Palestinian territory. While the world sees this as a political issue, there are unseen forces that drive both Israel's occupation and the strong hatred that is felt for them. Scripture suggests that the nation of Israel will one day play a major role in a war, in which the forces of Satan will line up against the forces of God in what will be the ultimate showdown on earth. Israel is clearly a strategic part of God's final battle with Satan.

God chose Israel to deliver His champion to the battle field:

The last reason is the most important. God used the nation of Israel to deliver His champion to the battle field. This topic requires special coverage and is the subject of a later chapter, entitled "The Lion Of Judah."

Our next stop is to examine how God changes His strategy from passive to aggressive in our next chapter "The Creator Strikes Back".

CHAPTER 6

THE CREATOR STRIKES BACK

It would seem that while the devil has been fairly aggressive in this battle so far, God appears to have been forced on the defensive. If you remember, the conflict started with Lucifer initiating an attack in an attempt to seize God's Throne. God responded by expelling him from heaven. The scene then shifted to the earth where God created man, gave him dominion over every living creature and appointed him guardian of Eden. Satan attacked God's creation and wrecked it all with sin. He scored a major victory in Eden and man is now eternally separated from God. God attempted to establish a foothold in a sin infected world and chose a people to Himself. Satan enslaved the Israelites in Egypt, engaged them in constant battle, incited them to rebel against God and attempted to eradicate them from the earth. It would appear that Satan has had things pretty much his way up to this point.

Let us examine what has happened so far in the context of modern day business tactics. As we have discussed before, in the real world of aggressive business competition, it sometimes happens that one company would initiate a deliberate hostile move against another. This often involves an attempt to "take over" or acquire the target company. At other times, it is an attempt to acquire strategic parts of the target company, like its market share, significant customers, key employees, or proprietary technology. Invariably, the owners of the opposing entities become locked in a battle of wits to see if either can achieve a strategic advantage, which would produce a financial benefit.

I have concluded after years of observing this type of behavior, that it is usually not the more aggressive or vocal entity that wins the contest, *but the one with the better strategy.*

God's defensive position probably raised some eyebrows in the angelic audience. What was God doing? Why was He allowing Satan to dictate the pace of the fight? God continued to fight for Israel down through the ages in an attempt to mold them into one nation under His banner. But every time He appeared to be making progress, Satan would break them apart by inciting them to sin which ultimately led them to be enslaved by other nations.

While God may appear to be constantly reacting to Satan's moves, I believe that He allowed Satan to dictate the pace of the early encounters in order to position him for a major counterstrike.

The Apostle Paul explained God's battle strategy this way:

> But when the fullness of the time had come, God sent forth His Son, born of a woman, born under the law to redeem those who were under the law, that we might receive the adoption as sons.
> (Galatians 4:4-5)

"When the fullness of time had come", God sent His champion. In other words, when God was good and ready, when the stage was set and when He was satisfied that everything was in place, *then* He changed tactics and launched a major offensive against the enemy. God apparently was waiting for some aspect of His plan to come to maturity before He responded with force.

So what was the basis of God's plan?

I believe that God was deliberately positioning and maneuvering Satan to take certain action that would ultimately lead to his downfall.

When Satan first started his campaign against man, he was very cunning, very cautious, very disguised. For example, he approached Eve in the form of a friendly charming snake. Eve never fully realized that she was in mortal danger and did not know who her attacker really was. Even when Satan attacked God's people, he would always motivate some human being to do his dirty deed. He used Pharaoh to enslave the Israelites and murder their children. While the person primarily held responsible for Egypt's cruelty to Israel was Pharaoh, clearly this work was inspired and instigated by the evil one.

All of the evil that has been acted out in the world, since the beginning of man's history, has been motivated and instigated by evil spirits under the direction of Satan their leader. Remember the angels who fought with Lucifer? Where do you think they are now, and what are they doing? They are an invisible presence, in the middle of man's affairs, instigating him to sin. This is the unseen war that I mentioned Satan is waging in our midst today.

Satan is the ultimate terrorist, remaining cleverly hidden behind the scenes, planning, coordinating and executing spiritual attacks on the entire human race, driving a wedge between man and God. He achieves his objectives by deceit and cunning, persuading human pawns to do his evil bidding. This strategy has now been adopted in the field of human conflict with lethal consequences.

Over the past decades the world has witnessed an upsurge in physical terrorism where men bent on evil, influence others to carry out acts of mass violence against unsuspecting people. Who do we ultimately hold accountable for terrorism whether spiritual or physical? The person doing the deed, or the person planning and coordinating the strategy?

Recent counter terrorism initiatives on a human level, suggest that the evil mastermind hiding behind the scenes *is the primary target* who must be found and neutralized in order to diminish the threat of future attacks.

In similar fashion, God's strategic plan must therefore, of necessity, find a way to draw Satan out from hiding and hold him accountable for the evil he has inflicted on mankind. But how does God achieve this? He does so by positioning Satan to expose himself as the murderer that he really is, **by catching him in the act.**

Up until this point in the battle between Satan and God, Satan hasn't directly or personally committed any crime against man. Yes he's motivated people to kill, *but he hasn't actually pulled the trigger himself.* In addition, every man who had died so far was worthy of death because of sin. But what if Satan were to actually, *personally* kill an innocent man? This, it turns out, is an important aspect of God's strategy to defeat him.

To see how God battle-tested and refined this tactic before Jesus came to earth in the flesh, let us take a look at Job from a slightly different perspective.

The trial of Job, revisited:

The obvious purpose of Job's trials is to show us an example of patient reliance on God in the midst of great difficulty. Job maintained godly integrity in the face of immense personal pressure, something we would all do well to emulate today. But consider how this encounter started:

> Now there was a day when the sons of God came to present themselves before the Lord, and Satan came also among them. And the Lord said unto Satan, "From where do you come?" So Satan answered the Lord and said, "From going to and fro in the earth and walking back and forth on it". Then the Lord said unto Satan, "Have you considered my servant Job, that there is none like him on the earth, a blameless and upright man, one that fears God and shuns evil?" So Satan answered the Lord and said, "Does Job fear God for nothing? Have you not made a hedge around him, around his household and around all that he has on every side? You have blessed the work of his hands, and his possessions have increased in the land. But now, stretch out Your hand and touch all that he has, and he will surely curse You to Your face!" And the Lord said to Satan, "Behold, all that he has is in your power; only do not lay a hand on his person". So Satan went from the presence of the Lord. (Job 1:6-12)

The day started like any other. The sons of God (presumably angelic beings) were making their accustomed appearance before the Throne of God. This time, Satan came in with them. Although Satan was not a "son of God", he was evidently allowed access to God's presence and apparently came before God occasionally to engage in a battle of wits. After the initial pleasantries sometimes exchanged between sworn enemies, God takes the initiative to engage Satan in discussion. In Job 1:8 God asks Satan, "Have you considered my servant Job (as a person of interest)?"

Now stop and think about poor Job for a minute. He has no clue that this conversation is taking place in the heavens. Here he is on earth, minding his own business, living a righteous life, being the perfect example of a Godly man and then, *God* points him out to Satan as a potential target.

But it gets worse for Job. God doesn't just point him out, but starts boasting about him being "blameless (or righteous) and upright", "one who fears God and shuns evil", "none like him in all the earth".

What are you doing God? *Trying to get Job killed??*

Sure enough Satan takes the bait. "Oh yeah? Job only acts righteously because you protect him. Lift Your protection over him and I will get him to curse You to Your face!". Satan is now committed to an act of direct confrontation with a man whom *God* declared to be righteous.

With God's consent, Satan destroys all of Job's possessions including his children. Job doesn't know what to make of the sudden spate of major disasters coming at him from all angles. First the Sabeans kill most of his servants and take away his oxen and asses. Then "the fire of God" as the news-bearer described it, falls from heaven and burns up all his sheep. Next, the Chaldeans seize all of his camels and kill the remainder of his servants. Worst of all, his children were at one brother's house and a great wind destroys the house and kills them all. What an unbelievable catastrophe. Job loses every thing in the blink of an eye.

This is an investor's worst nightmare. The stock market crashes, the housing market collapses, your house is destroyed, you lose your job, your banker has *made-off* with all your savings. Every thing you have worked for and built up over the last 40 years is gone. It is not difficult to envisage someone experiencing even a part of a tragedy like this exploding in anger and letting loose a few choice words aimed at heaven. In addition to the frustration of his financial loss, Job also has to deal with the grief of the deaths of his children. Satan waits to see if Job will shake his fist at God as he predicted. But this is not what happens at all. Rather than curse God, Job falls to his knees and blesses and worships his creator, in the midst of his anguish and pain.

> Then Job arose, tore his robe, and shaved his head: and fell to the ground and worshiped. And he said, "Naked came I from my mother's womb and naked I shall return there. The Lord gave and the Lord has taken away; Blessed be the name if the Lord."
> (Job 1:20-21)

Job passes the test with flying colors. Satan must have been highly annoyed by this. Not only are the angels of heaven looking on, but so are his demons. Job is making him look bad in front of his boys! Even more determined now to destroy Job, Satan goes back to God.

Job 2: 1-8 tells us that Satan presents himself before God for a second time. God acknowledges him and asks the same question as He did before: "From where do you come?" Now God knew fully well where Satan was and what he had done to Job, but again, He was about to egg Satan on even further. God repeats the same glowing comments about Job, but this time, possibly with a little smile on His face (so to speak). Here is what I think God's comments may have sounded like in Satan's hearing:

"Satan have you considered My servant Job, how he is blameless and upright and how he respects Me completely? Now, the last time you were here, *you* told Me, that if I gave you authority to destroy all his possessions, he would curse Me to my face. Well, instead of him cursing Me, he's praising My name and worshiping Me. Look, look, Satan, there he is right now. See what I told you? *That* is My beloved servant Job, in whom I am well pleased."

Satan responds:

> So Satan answered the Lord and said, "Skin for skin! Yes, all that a man has he will give for his life.
> But stretch out your hand now, and touch his bone and his flesh and he will curse You to Your face"
> (Job 2:4)

Now this is getting *really* serious. Satan is asking God for permission to torture Job to the point of death. His murderous comment is: "All that a man has he will give for his life." Satan is talking about torturing Job until he either curses God or dies.

Remember that Satan does not have any authority over Job that God does not grant. Job is a righteous man in God's eyes and has lived his life so far, completely under the protection of God. Because of God's hedge (Job 1:10) around Job, no force of evil, including the devil himself could touch him. So Satan ramps it up. "Give me power to inflict pain and suffering on Job up to the point of death and I will make him curse you to your face."

In an act of divine strategy, God places Job's life in Satan's hands to do as he sees fit. The only restraint that God imposes on Satan is that he cannot take Job's life.

This is a very significant strategic move by God. Satan was so incensed by God's faith in Job and Job's loyalty to God, that he was prepared to kill an innocent man. God declares Job to be a "blameless and upright man" in His eyes and yet the devil has no hesitation in killing him. Satan never had to ask permission to kill Job's servants or his children because they were not righteous in the eyes of God, but sinners and subject to death. Only Job was under a hedge of protection created by God.

This is where Job's story fits in to God's eternal plan. I believe that God used Job to draw out Satan's true nature and commit him to the point of being willing to shed innocent blood, *and then, held him back*.

We know how the story of Job ends. Satan inflicts Job with painful boils from the crown of his head to the soles of his feet. He sends his friends and his wife to torment Job and persuade him to curse God and die. Yet Job maintains his integrity before God. God restores to Job all that he lost and more, in honor of his faithfulness and loyalty. There is only one other man apart from Job, whom God declared to be righteous and whom Satan *personally* attempted to kill and that is Jesus of Nazareth.

Satan reigned on the earth for many thousands of years after Job and continued his campaign of hatred and anger towards God's people, and in particular those who attempted to walk uprightly before God. During this time, he constantly monitors the utterances of the prophets to glean any strategic information about God's plan for man.

Amos 3:7 confirms:
"Surely the Lord does nothing, unless He reveals His secret unto His servants the prophets".

God's prophets have the job of declaring specific details of His strategic plan well in advance. The declarations of the prophets are like God's signature and spiritual finger print on the history of the world. They allow us, who come along after the fact, to look back and recognize His handiwork.

Satan knows that God is planning something big, but exactly what, is unclear to him. Then these very disturbing prophesies begin to emerge:

> "But you, Bethlehem Ephratath, though you are little among the thousands of Judah, yet out of you shall come forth to Me the One to be Ruler in Israel, whose goings forth are from old, from everlasting."
> (Micah 5:2)

> For unto us a Child is born, unto us a Son is given: and the government shall be upon His shoulder: and his name will be called Wonderful, Counselor, Mighty God, Everlasting Father, Prince of Peace. Of the increase of His government and peace there will be no end, upon the throne of David and upon His Kingdom to order it and to establish with judgment and justice from that time forward, even forever. The zeal of the Lord of hosts will perform this.
> (Isaiah 9:6-7)

> "Yet have I set My King upon My holy hill of Zion. I will declare the decree: the Lord has said to Me, You are my Son, today have I begotten You. Ask of Me and I will give You the nations for Your inheritance and the ends of the earth for Your possession".
> (Psalm 2:6-8)

All of a sudden (or so it seemed to Satan), God's prophets are abuzz with many messages like these. The key words identified in the prophesies are:

1. A child is born
2. Everlasting ruler

3. Upon the throne of David
4. to establish judgment and justice
5. the government shall be upon His shoulder
6. His name will be Wonderful, Counselor, *The mighty God*
7. You are my Son.
8. I will give You the nations for your inheritance and the ends of the earth for Your possession.

In one shocking moment, Satan and his underlings decipher the code and realize: ***The Son is coming.*** It could mean nothing else. God the Son, the Word, who created creation, is coming to earth. This must have tied a huge knot deep in Satan's stomach.

Not only is the Son coming, but His intentions are clear. The Creator is about to strike back.

> Indeed He says, "It is too small a thing that You should be My Servant to raise up the tribes of Jacob and to restore the preserved Israel; I will also give You as a light to the Gentiles that You should be my salvation unto the ends of the earth".
> (Isaiah 49:6)

What!! Raise up the tribes of Jacob?? Restore Israel?? Salvation to the Gentiles to the ends of the earth???

Satan realized then that God was about to launch a direct attack against him and that God's Son, The Prince Of Peace would soon arrive on the earth to do battle. Satan's likely position would have been, "If He comes into my domain, to take from me what is legally mine, *I will kill Him*".

So, the fullness of time has come and the battle is about to begin in earnest. All of creation will soon be focused on the life of a Jewish carpenter, Jesus of Nazareth.

The Lion of the Tribe of Judah is about to enter the arena to do battle with the dragon. Unlike the first encounter between Lucifer and the forces of God, this was not going to be a war among angelic beings in the heavens (Revelation 12:7), but a physical battle on the earth, *in which blood would be shed and people would die.*

It is time now to go behind the scenes of each camp and consider the strategies adopted by each as they prepare for battle, first by examining the dragon's tactics and then the Lion's. Up next, we "Enter the dragon's lair".

CHAPTER 7

ENTER THE DRAGON'S LAIR

As we have seen, Satan understands that God's word is a declaration of His will, so he constantly monitors the words of the prophets for signs of God's divine plan for man. The many prophecies about the birth of a redeemer, the Son of God dwelling among men, suggested that God intended to come to earth in the flesh and initiate some sort of spiritual revival or uprising among men.

Satan would have realized that if the Word became flesh, God would be able to communicate directly with man, which would be far more effective than speaking through the prophets. Perhaps God's plan was that the Word would come to earth and lead mankind out of spiritual slavery, like Moses did with the Isrealites in Egypt. Maybe the ultimate intention was that God would set up a kingdom on the earth in the midst of Satan's domain, where men could find a place of refuge and live under His protection.

Certainly, if that was in fact what God was planning, the

devil was not about to sit idly by and just let it happen.
So what was Satan's plan to stop Jesus, the Word made flesh?

Satan defeated Adam by cunning and stealth and he must have fancied his chances against Adam's apparent replacement. Victory in this battle would put an end to any further attempt by God to destabilize his rule on the earth and would seal the fate of man eternally. Not only would the earth be under his full control, but if the Word could be tempted to sin, then the Godhead would be invalidated. This could provide a way for the devil to secure his original objective of laying claim to God's throne. Satan realized that God coming to the earth "in the flesh" opened up definite strategic opportunities for him.

But what strategy would best achieve Satan's objectives?

His plan was to employ a two point attack against Jesus. Here are his options:

1. Assassinate Jesus and terminate God's plan before it could come to fruition.

2. Trick the man Jesus in to sin like he did with Adam and make Him subject to death like all other men.

Having determined his best options, what the devil needed now was to find the right opportunity to strike. It wasn't too long before such an opening presented itself:

Option 1: The plot to kill Jesus

Now the birth of Jesus Christ was as follows: After His mother Mary was betrothed to Joseph, before they came

together, she was found with child of the Holy Spirit.
(Matthew 1: 18)

The first two chapters of the book of Matthew provide us with the details of the most celebrated birth in all the world. History remembers famous people such as great leaders, politicians, religious figures, scientists, explorers, because of their achievements and contributions to society. No one, however, pays much attention to the detailed circumstances surrounding their birth.

Yet the birth of this baby to poor Jewish parents, two thousand years ago, is celebrated in different cultures, countries and languages, even today. The birth of the Savior is commemorated every year with songs of joy and worship such as: "Joy to the world", "O Holy night", "Do you hear what I hear", "The first Noel", and "Hark the herald angels sing".

Although we sing songs like these every year, we never grow tired of them because they evoke strong emotions of gratitude that God sent the savior. But lurking behind the scenes of this time of *"peace, goodwill toward men"* (Luke 2:14), was a very sinister plot.

Matthew chapter 2 tells us that, just around the time of Jesus' birth, a delegation of foreign diplomats, or wise men, paid a visit to Herod, King of Judea. They told him that they were seeking a baby who was born "King of the Jews". This was very disturbing news for Herod. The birth of someone claiming to be Jewish royalty, was an affront to his reign and could ultimately undermine Roman rule.

Herod was seething with anger, but he maintained his composure in the presence of the wise men, because he needed their help to find the child. He could not allow this baby to grow up and lay claim to his throne, or lead the Jews in rebellion against Rome. This child had to be found and put to death *immediately.* This is how Satan manipulates evil men to do his bidding on the earth. He determines what he wants done then finds a human whose interests are aligned with his and who would be willing to act out his evil intent. Herod's plan to kill the baby to secure his own political future was in fact a demonic suggestion planted by Satan to achieve his primary objective of finding and killing Jesus.

Matthew 2:4 tells us that Herod summons the chief priests and scribes and demands that they tell him where the Christ would be born. Although the scribes and priests were religious leaders they were also important representatives of the Jewish people under Roman rule. The last thing *they* wanted was someone claiming to be King of the Jews upsetting their Roman masters and causing problems for them.

So, to appease Herod, they confirmed that the ruler of Israel would be born in Bethlehem. They knew that Herod was a ruthless man, who would not hesitate to kill this baby. But, as Caiaphas the chief priest would point out some thirty-three years later, "it is better for one man to die than for the whole nation to perish" (John 11:50.)

Now the interests of Satan, Rome *and* the Jewish religious rulers were all permanently aligned. They all wanted this baby (and later this Man) dead for different reasons. In establishing this alliance with Rome and the Jewish priests, Satan put in place the infrastructure to kill Jesus. This was going to happen, it was only a matter of time.

Herod dispatched the wise men to Bethlehem and told them to let him know when they found the baby, so he too could pay his respects. But they were warned of Herod's murderous intent and kept Jesus' location secret from him.

When Herod realized that the wise men had tricked him he ordered the slaughter of every child in Bethlehem and the surrounding districts, under the age of two just to make sure that this King did not survive. Satan wasn't about to lose the opportunity to strike the first blow.

Today we sing "O little town of Bethlehem" in joyous reverence to the place of the Savior's birth. The harsh reality is, however, as Matthew 2:18 tells us, there were hundreds maybe thousands of parents weeping over the bodies of their slaughtered babies in Bethlehem. Had it not been for God's warning to the wise men and to Joseph, the manger would have been another crime scene. Herod's plot in Bethlehem was the first of many attempts instigated by Satan to kill Jesus. Here are some of the others:

Luke 4: 28-29
Jesus was teaching in the synagogue in His home town of Nazareth. The people recognized Him as a "local boy" and took offense that He should be speaking to them with such authority. "Is this not Joseph's son?" In other words, "who does *he* think he is?"

Jesus points the finger back at them, saying, "No prophet is accepted in his own country." This infuriates the crowd and they seize Jesus, take Him outside of the city, intending to throw Him head first over a cliff. Jesus had to conceal Himself to escape.

John 5:18
Jesus was in Jerusalem and heals a lame man by the pool of Bethesda on the Sabbath. He explains that His authority to heal comes from Him being God. This infuriates the Jews and makes them even more determined to kill Him.

John 8: 58-59

Jesus goes into the temple at the Mount of Olives and in explaining who He was, makes the statement: "Before Abraham was, I am." Immediately the Jews take up stones to kill Him.

John 10: 30-33

Jesus was in Jerusalem during the Feast of the Dedication and goes into the temple in Solomon's porch. There He makes the statement "I and my Father are one". Immediately,"the Jews took up stones again to stone him" (vs 31).

After many failed attempts on His life, Jesus is eventually betrayed by one of His inner circle, captured like a wanted criminal and condemned to die.

> Now the Feast of Unleavened Bread drew near, which is called Passover. And the chief priests and scribes sought how they might kill Him, for they feared the people. Then entered Satan into Judas, surnamed Iscariot, who was numbered among the twelve. So he went his way and conferred with the chief priests and captains, how he might betray Him unto them. And they were glad, and agreed to give him money.
> (Luke 22: 1-5)

The chief priests badly wanted to kill Jesus for two main reasons. His growing popularity with the people could position Him to lead a rebellion against Roman rule. According to John 6:15, at one time there was even an attempt by some with political intent to take Jesus by force and make Him king. The other, and probably more urgent reason, was that Jesus had claimed to be the Son of God and on more than one occasion exposed their hypocrisy, challenged their authority, condemned their sacred laws and revealed their sin. No doubt they were desperate to kill

Jesus, but were reluctant to seize Him for fear of the people who counted Him as a prophet of God. The priests seem stuck, unsure of how to proceed and too timid to take risks. Satan decided that this had gone on long enough and was no longer prepared to leave it to incompetent, indecisive men to get the job done. He intervenes personally, enters into Judas and uses him as a catalyst to deliver Jesus to death.

Up until this time, the devil had played an unseen role in the murder plot, staying behind the scenes as a silent instigator. But now, there was a sense of urgency in his camp and he was forced to adopt the "If you want something done properly, *do it yourself*" approach.

By entering into Judas, Satan, who was positively identified in the above passage of scripture (*"then entered Satan into Judas"*), steps out of the shadows and takes a direct hand in the death of Jesus. Within short order, his mission is accomplished. Jesus is arrested, tortured by flogging and is on His way to the cross. Not exactly the sort of ending the devil was hoping for, but at least this puts an end to Jesus building His kingdom on the earth.

Option 2: Trick Jesus to commit sin

Strategically, the *best result* for Satan would have been to *first* trap Jesus in sin and *then* put Him to death. If he could get Jesus to sin, then game over. Jesus would be subject to spiritual death like all men and therefore fully under Satan's control. This is Satan's most powerful weapon against mankind and it was the one he was relying on to end the battle decisively in his favor.

Matthew chapter 4 tells us that this is exactly what Satan set out to do in the wilderness, tempt Jesus to sin using proven methods that he, Satan had perfected on men for thousands of years. Remember that this is how he trapped Eve in the garden, by twisting what God had said and getting her to obey his lie rather than God's truth. In Eden, Eve faced the tempter alone, face-to-face, without the intervention of the Father. So did Jesus when the Spirit led him into His own version of Eden, the wilderness, to face the devil.

In this segment we will examine the temptation in the wilderness from the point of view of Satan's strategy to trick Jesus and trap Him in sin. In a later chapter we will consider the same passages of scripture, but from the point of view of Jesus' strategy to defeat Satan. Unknown to Satan at the time, the temptation in the wilderness was not really about him testing Jesus, but more about Jesus testing him. Remember that it was *the Spirit* that led Jesus into the wildernesses to be tempted. This was God's agenda, not Satan's. The purpose, as we shall see was not to determine if Jesus could withstand the devil, *but rather, if the devil could withstand Jesus.*

> Then Jesus was led up by the Spirit into the wilderness to be tempted by the devil. And when he had fasted forty days and forty nights, afterward He was hungry. Now when the tempter came to him, he said, "If you are the Son of God, command that these stones become bread."
> (Matthew 4:1-3)

Satan's tactic was to challenge Jesus in three specific areas: **His identity** (*"If thou be the son of God"*), **His humanity** (*"command that these stones be made bread"*) and **His loyalty** (*"fall down and worship me"*)

Let us examine each of these in turn:

His identity: *"If thou be the Son of God".*
Satan most likely would have been present at the baptism of Jesus and would have heard the Father say "This is my

beloved Son in whom I am well pleased" (Matthew 3:17). Jesus' identity was going to be the basis of the first challenge by the devil. Satan's initial approach to Jesus was not confrontational, but with the same subtle conversational style he used on Eve back in Genesis 3:1 *"didn't God say that you can eat of every tree in the garden?"*

The tempter's cunning approach was, in essence, "Look Jesus, I heard the Father say that you're the Son. Now, I don't mean to raise this as an issue, but is it *really* you? You look different. If you're in fact the Son of God, *prove it to me"*.

Fallen man has this quirk of always wanting to prove or justify ourselves when we think we are right. It is something I believe that flows out of pride and arrogance. We always want to have the last word. If someone challenges us on some issue, rather than let God be true and every man a liar, we want to prove that *we* are right and *they* are wrong, which often leads to anger, debate and strife. Satan was attempting to press what he thought were Jesus' buttons. If he could get the Son to obey his demand for proof of ID, then Jesus would have subordinated His will and authority to the devil.

As an example, in a traffic stop, when a law enforcement officer demands proof of identification, you obediently produce your driver's license for scrutiny. By so doing, you are in fact recognizing the officer's lawful authority over you and you are submitting your will to that authority by compliance. This is what Satan was after in Jesus, submission and compliance.

Jesus wasn't about to fall into that trap. He didn't have anything to prove to Satan or to the world. He was who God said He was. We would do well to remember that. We are, who God says we are. There is no spiritual need to prove ourselves to anyone else. Have you ever heard this before? "You call yourself a Christian? If you were *really* a

Christian, then you would (or wouldn't) do this or say that!" Does that sound familiar? Don't let the devil or the world tell you who you are. Jesus said (Matthew 6:17) that it is by our fruit that we are known. Let the fruit of the Spirit identify you for who you are.

His humanity: *"Command that these stones be made bread."*

I have never fasted for 40 days and nights, but I would imagine that after such a long period without food, Jesus would have been physically weak, with His body in survival mode and crying out for nourishment. Some bread would have been exactly what the devil ordered. Elected officials know that the use of appointed authority for personal gain is an act of fraud. Similarly, Satan was attempting to get Jesus to commit divine fraud by using His supernatural power to gratify His flesh.

How many times have we allowed our bodies or our appetites to cause us to make decisions that we knew were contrary to God's word or ways? To succeed in His mission, Jesus had to live a sinless life, which means that He had to conquer the passions of His own body and put them under subjection to God's word. The same applies to us. None of us is perfect, but the Apostle Paul tells us:

> Therefore brethren, we are debtors not to the flesh to live according to the flesh. For if you live according to the flesh you will die; but if by the Spirit you put to death the deeds of the body, you will live. For as many as are led by the Spirit of God, these are the sons of God.
> (Romans 8: 12-14)

According to Romans 8, if we live according to the dictates of our flesh, we will die spiritually, because we will be yielding our bodies to sin. If, however, we bring our bodies under subjection to the Spirit of God, God's life will take root in us and the Holy Spirit will lead us as sons (of both sexes) towards our individual destinies. This is what Jesus was demonstrating here for our benefit, how to submit ourselves to God and allow Him to lead us "in the paths of righteousness for His name's sake" (Psalm 23:3).

His loyalty: *"fall down and worship me".*

> Again the devil took Him up on an exceedingly high mountain, and showed Him all the kingdoms of the world and the glory. And said to Him, "All these things I will give You if You will fall down and worship me."
> (Matthew 4: 8-9)

In this last temptation, Satan comes out from hiding, abandons all subtlety and gets right down to business. Satan's last act of desperation was to attempt to bribe Jesus by offering Him all the kingdoms of the world in exchange for His loyalty. It was a simple transaction, "I will give you all these things Jesus, if you will bow down and worship me". Jesus said in Matthew 6:24 that no-one can serve two masters. We have to give our loyalty to either God *or* the devil. We can't be loyal to both and whenever we declare ourselves to be the people of God, expect the tempter to turn up and offer some incentive to get us to turn our back on God's principles or His ways, as he did with Eve.

The offer made to Jesus is still being made to us today, but with more subtlety. The glory of the world is not just about wealth, but also about fame, popularity, fan worship, power, "respect" and other ego stroking accolades. Most of us would like to think that we would not sell our souls for riches and fame and we would certainly never bow to Satan.

Satan knows that God's people will reject any direct offer of wealth or fame in exchange for submission to evil. A grounded Christian will recognize a bribe for what it is, *a direct offer from the devil to sell his/her integrity for financial gain*, and will not bow to this. For such people the devil uses what I call the "indirect method". What he does, is offer us a little incentive (e.g. the praise of an employer) to make a small compromise. Once we bite this fruit, he offers us another little incentive much later on, long after we have forgotten the first offer to compromise.

Every time we fall prey to this, we bow a little lower. The process is so gradual that it is only after much time has passed and we look back to where we started, we realize that we are no longer walking upright but with a stoop. One of my favorite radio preachers in the 1980's, Pastor Dan Betzer, called this "The deceptiveness of the gradual".

Here are some examples of how this works in practice.

1) You find at the end of the year that you owe the IRS taxes (or you would like to get a bigger refund) and your tax preparer tells you he/she can "fix things" so you pay less taxes (or get more money back). My advice, *find another tax preparer.* Tax evasion is not only a crime, it is an offense to God. Many years ago, a certain CPA was asked a question by a taxpayer about his obligation to pay federal taxes. After examining the currency in question, the CPA said:

> "Render therefore unto Caesar the things that are Caesar's, and unto God the things that are God's."
> (Matthew 22:21)

Sounds like good business advice to me.

2) The cashier at the store gives you extra change by mistake. This is not a blessing from God, but a test from the tempter. God requires us to act with integrity in all things and would expect us to:

> "Have regard for good things in the sight of all men" (Romans 12:17).

The appropriate response would be to give back the excess change, no matter how small.

3) Your boss asks you to tell a "little white lie" to appease a customer. You respectfully decline, even if it means that you don't get that promotion you were hoping for. In my opinion, it is better to be promoted by a righteous God than a crooked boss.

4) You mess up in some way and an opportunity arises for you to blame someone else for your error without being discovered. Don't fall for that. Ask the Lord to help you out of your trouble, but be prepared to take responsibility for your actions. Never be tempted to lay the blame for your mistake, no matter how small, on someone else.

These are the somewhat tough decisions we must make if we want to walk uprightly before the Lord. Our response in such situations must always be, "Satan, I recognize your attempt to pervert me. Get away from me!"

There is in my opinion, an important difference between a trial and a temptation.

A trial results in a test of our faith, and is usually the result of some challenge we face in life in which God wants us to trust Him in spite of the hardship before us or obstacles that stand in our way. A good example of this would be Shadrach, Meshach and Abednego, the three Jewish boys of Daniel 3:12, who faced certain death for refusing to bow down to a pagan king. The trial of their faith was to either bow, or burn. The trial of faith faced by some in the early church was to either renounce Jesus, or be fed to the lions. Our trial today may be some financial need that forces us to depend on God as our provider, a health issue for which we must believe God for healing, or any number of similar situations in which we have to trust God for a solution.

A temptation on the other hand is a situation where *bait is dangled* before us as an inducement or incentive to do something wrong or evil (lie, cheat, steal, inflict hurt, kill and so on). The tempter (whom I believe to be a high ranking Satanic spirit), is a predator, *a hunter of souls,* and the believer is his intended prey. Here is what Peter says about his approach and strategy:

> Be sober, be vigilant; because your adversary the devil walks about like a roaring lion, seeking whom he may devour.
> (1 Peter 5:8)

The tempter's approach is to encourage us to gratify the flesh, or pursue some personal agenda in a manner contrary to God's word or ways. It is important to understand that God does not tempt us with evil or bait us to sin:

> Let no one say when he is tempted, "I am tempted of God"; for God cannot be tempted by evil, nor does He tempt anyone.
> (James1:13)

Satan is the author of temptation and his plan is to wreck

our faith and destroy our testimony. God *allows* trials in our lives and His plan is to build our faith and give us a testimony:

> My brethren, count it all joy when you fall into various trials, knowing that the testing of your faith produces patience.
> (James 1:2-3)

Once we can make the distinction between trial and temptation, we will, like the Lord Jesus, be able to discern the source of the things that come against us, and decide which of these two will be our response: "Father, I will trust you to the end", or "Get away from me Satan".

Satan made many other attempts to test, distract, and defeat Jesus during His mission to earth, most of them aimed at the frailty of His human flesh. Some people wonder how could Jesus be subject to temptation if He was God, and God cannot be tempted with sin (James 1:13). What we must bear in mind is that while on earth, Jesus was God *in the flesh.*

In his divine form, nothing can tempt or threaten God. God does not feel anxiety, fear, insecurity, rejection as we do. For Jesus to be that perfect substitute for us on the cross and to qualify as our High Priest, He had to overcome all these human emotions and frailties *and remain sinless.* In those lonely final hours before His crucifixion, as He contemplated the horror of the cross, His human frailty cried out to the Father: "Father, if it is at all possible, let this cup pass from Me", then His God-nature, driven by His sense of divine purpose, responds for Him, "Nevertheless, not My will, but thy will be done".

Here is how the Apostle Paul explains Jesus being tempted in the flesh:

> For we do not have a High Priest who cannot sympathize with our weakness, but was in all points tempted as we are yet without sin. (Hebrews 4:15)

The challenge that Jesus faced on the earth was not so much how to outwit Satan, but how to live as a human, in complete submission to the Father, and not yield to His flesh at any time for any reason. At the end of the day, Satan was not successful in getting the Son of God to compromise or to sin, so the only way to stop Him, *was to kill Him.* As we shall see, this might not have been such a good idea after all.

Now that we have considered the dragon's battle plan, let us consider the Lion's strategy to conquer the enemy.

Up next, The Lion of the Tribe of Judah has His say.

CHAPTER 8

THE LION OF THE TRIBE OF JUDAH

We have just concluded our examination of Satan's strategy to defeat God's champion, the Lion. In this chapter we will look deeper into God's plan in sending His Son to the earth and His battle strategy against the powers of darkness. As we saw earlier, Satan adopted the same strategy against Jesus in the wilderness, that he applied against Eve in the garden. His approach was to use subtlety and cunning persuasion, to present reasonable arguments, some backed by scripture quotations, to entice Jesus to sin.

Satan realized from this experience that Jesus was far more formidable than the first Adam, and that He acted with the very authority and composure of God. Jesus allowed Satan to throw the first punch in the wilderness. Now it was His turn to respond.

The Apostle John confirms that:

> For this purpose the Son of God was manifested, that He might destroy the works of the devil.
> (1 John 3:8)

Jesus came to earth to do two things:

- Destroy the works of the devil;

- Free man from the ravages of sin and death.

God intended to destroy that is, put an end to the devil's work by attacking and smashing it into pieces. In the encounter in the book of Job, God seemed willing to engage Satan in dialogue and a battle of wits. **Now that the Lion had entered the arena, those days were over.** There would no longer be any room for negotiation or discussion with the devil. This was to be a battle to the death, where there would be only one winner. Jesus was here to impose dominion in the earth and to rip the devil's world apart. Before we take a closer look at God's battle plan let us review what we know about the Messiah that the prophets promised would come.

Each of us has a different image, or relationship identity, based on the perspective of the person looking at us. For example, I am Robert. To my wife Jacqueline, I am her husband. To my children, I am their father. To my parents, I am their son. To my daughter's dog, I am the enemy. To my clients, I am their adviser. To all of these people, I am someone different by relationship, but to me, I am just Robert.

Similarly, Jesus can be seen from different perspectives depending on our vantage point:

- As the creator in the beginning, He is the *"Word"* (John 1:1);

- At the point of transition to a human person, He is the *"Word made flesh"* (John 1:14);

- As an expression of His absolute humanity, He is the *"Son of man"* (Mark 10; 45);

- As the promised Messiah, He is Emmanuel, *God with us* (Matthew 1:23);

- As our master, He is *Jesus Christ, our Lord* (Philippians 2:11);

- To the Church, He is the *Bridegroom* (2 Corinthians 11:2);

- As our sacrifice, he is the *"Lamb that was slain"* (Revelation 5:6);

And, as God's champion, He is the ***"Lion of the Tribe of Judah."***

> Then I saw a strong angel proclaim with a loud voice, "Who is worthy to open the book, and to loose the seals?" And no one in heaven nor in earth or under the earth was able to open the scroll, or to look at it. And I wept much, because no one was found worthy to open and read the scroll, or to look at it. But one of the elders said to me, "Do not weep. Behold, the Lion of the tribe of Judah, the Root of David

has prevailed to open the scroll and to loose its seven seals."
(Revelation 5:2-5)

This passage of scripture from the book of Revelation, jumps us ahead to the conclusion of God's plan for man. It identifies Jesus, the Lion of Judah, as the only one worthy to take the book from the right hand of God (Rev. 5:7) and open it. The book of Revelation seems to be giving us a front row seat at the awards ceremony of the ages, where the champion steps forward to claim the ultimate prize, a book with seven seals.

But what is this prize, and why is Jesus the only one deemed worthy to claim it? The contents of this book or scroll, have been subject to much discussion by Bible scholars over the years. Some authorities suggest that the scroll contains the title deed to the earth, or that it was the final will and testament of God concerning the universe.

While I am by no means a Bible scholar, from our layman's analysis of God's strategic agenda, I believe that this document was in fact a proclamation of man's emancipation from slavery to sin, in the form of **a discharged judgment lien**. A 'judgment lien' is a document issued by the court that gives a creditor, someone that you owe, the legal right to seize your property and dispose of it to satisfy your debt.

This lien, or claim against the souls of all men, expresses God's righteous judgment for sin and the sentence of death to all men, because all have sinned. Then, I believe, written somewhere in that scroll, is a declaration that the judgment for sin was satisfied through payment rendered in person by the 'Lamb that was slain".

Revelation 5 appears to be more than just an awards ceremony. *It may in fact be a court session in progress in the heavens.* The court was called to order by the strong angel asking, "Who is worthy to open the book?" before the Righteous Judge sitting on the throne and the defendant man, (possibly represented by the weeping John??) in attendance. When no one was found worthy to open the book, John wept, because he knew the consequence for all men. Then one of the elders present, comforted John with words to this effect: "Don't cry John, man isn't doomed. Look, the Champion, the Lion of the Tribe of Judah, He has prevailed and is worthy to open the book. *Man has been redeemed!"*

From the moment sin, and death by sin, infected mankind, **God's number one strategic priority was to find a cure, or solution to redeem man.** Jesus' primary objective in coming to the earth was to save man from sin. God sums up Jesus' mission to earth in this declaration of purpose:

> "For God so loved the world that He gave His only begotten Son that whosoever believes in Him should not perish but have everlasting life. For God did not send His Son into the world to condemn the world, but that the world through Him might be saved."
> (John 3:16-17)

This is the fulfillment of God's contract made with Abraham thousands of years before. Abraham's willingness to sacrifice his own son in obedience to God, provided the right of way for God to reciprocate by sending Jesus. But before Jesus could emancipate man, He first had to do battle with the enemy standing in His way. In this role, He is seen as the Lion of the Tribe of Judah. This is where we now pick up the action.

Enter the Lion:

> And when He was baptized, Jesus came up immediately from the water; and behold, the heavens were opened to

Him, and He saw the Spirit of God descending like a dove and alighting upon him. And suddenly a voice came from heaven saying, "This is my beloved Son in whom I am well pleased." Then was Jesus led up by the Spirit into the wilderness to be tempted by the devil. (Matthew 3:16-4:1)

This is the start of Jesus' ministry, or rather, His active engagement of the devil in the battlefield. The battle starts in the same way that it did for Job, with the introduction of heaven's champion. In the battle of Job, God tells the devil that Job was His man in the earth, righteous, upstanding, a worthy adversary.

When God thundered "This is my beloved Son, in whom I Am well pleased" at Jesus' baptism, He was, to my mind, announcing that the battle was about to begin "for real" and His Son was entering the arena. This was the heavyweight championship of the world and God's warrior had been announced by heaven. Immediately after this announcement was made, scripture tells us that Jesus was "led up by the Spirit into the wilderness to be tempted of the devil". Jesus did not wait for the devil to come looking for Him, He, led by the Spirit, *went looking for the devil.* From this point on, the battle was about to change.

Until now, the dragon has been having things pretty much his way. He tormented Job, killed the prophets, slaughtered countless babies hunting for Moses and Jesus and inflicted unimaginable horror on man, including sickness, pain, fear, demonic possession and death.

By stepping out into the wilderness to challenge Satan, the Lion was about to launch a massive assault on the devil and his angels, which would drive fear and terror into their hearts and from which they would never recover. This was no "gentle Jesus meek and mild", but a righteous God with a very big sword, about to do major damage to the kingdom of darkness.

The first difference that Satan noticed, was Jesus' response to his temptation to satisfy His hunger. After not eating for so long, most of us would have at least flirted with the tempter's invitation to eat some nice, warm, home made bread. The more we thought about that bread, the more we could actually smell and taste it. Our senses and appetite would take over and pretty soon we would be going berserk trying to turn the stone into bread, as the tempter suggested. James explains the process of temptation to us:

> But each one is tempted when he is drawn away by his own desires and enticed. Then when desire has conceived, it gives birth to sin: and sin, when it is full grown brings forth death.
> (James 1:14-15)

We could not ask for a more accurate, clearer description, of what the tempter was trying to do to Jesus. Use hunger, which is a legitimate human bodily need, to lead Him from desire to sin to death. By suggesting that He turn the stones into bread, Satan was attempting to get Jesus to use His supernatural power to satisfy the demands of the flesh. In addition as we saw in the previous chapter, the tempter was also trying to get Jesus to bow to him and prove His identity, a sort of "killing two birds with one stone" strategy.

But the Lion would have none of this. After listening politely to the offer, Jesus responded simply:

> "It is written, Man shall not live by bread alone, but by every word that proceeds from the mouth of God."
> (Matthew 4:4)

Huh?

This is the first time, in recorded history, that a man has stood up to the devil with boldness and confidence and declared, "This is what God's word has to say about your offer". The Lion had just introduced the devil to the latest in weapon technology, the living Word, which is the sword of the Spirit. The tempter, in a state of shock, takes another crack at the Lion. This time, he shows great skill and adaptation, by using the same words "for it is written" in formulating his temptation hypothesis and quoting scripture just as Jesus had done:

> Then the devil took Him up into the holy city, set Him on the pinnacle of the temple, and said unto Him, "If You are the Son of God, throw yourself down. For it is written: 'He shall give his angels charge over you' and 'In their hands they shall bear you up, Lest you dash your foot against a stone.'"
> (Matthew 4:5-6)

Now if this weren't such a serious matter it would be truly comical. Imagine the devil quoting Psalm 91, using Scripture, *Jesus' own sword* against Him. Jesus puts a swift end to that nonsense.

> Jesus said unto him, "It is written again, You shall not tempt the Lord your God."
> (Matthew 5:7)

What Jesus was in effect saying to the tempter was: "Listen to me devil, I am not playing games with you. You shall not tempt the Lord your God, *Whom I am*. By even suggesting this to me, your are in violation of the word of God"

Huh???

Finally, the devil goes for broke and attempts to bribe Jesus with every thing he owns. "I will give you all the kingdoms of the world if you would fall down and worship me" (Matthew: 4:9). This time, Satan has stepped way over the line. Jesus calls him out by name for the first time in their encounter, "Away with you, Satan", and with a great whack of His sword, sends him running for cover.

From Satan's perspective, this was truly shocking. What just happened here? The Lion had just declared the new authority structure on earth, *"You shall worship the Lord your God and only Him shall you serve."* 2 Corinthians 4:4 tells us that Satan is the god of this world and that he blinds the minds of people and they follow him. The human race has been blindly bowing down to the devil, by allowing him to influence our decisions and dictate our actions. In his arrogance, Satan was telling Jesus "I am god of this world and I can give you anything you want, but you must bow to me".

The Lion's response to Satan was, "The days of your lordship in the earth are over. A higher authority is here and God's Kingdom has come. It is not me who should bow to you, **but it is *you* who must now bow to *me!*** Pack up and get out!" And with that, the devil was forced to leave. This is the first time that Satan and his demons ever felt fear in the presence of a man. Even with Job, there was no question of who was in control of the battle. Satan had no fear of Job. But this time, *there was fear.* Never before had they encountered anyone whom the tempter could not manipulate, outwit, entice, bully or bribe and who commanded the very authority of God by his word. The big concern for Satan now, is what would happen to the kingdom of darkness, if Jesus could teach other men to act in this way. Unfortunately for him, he was about to find out.

Immediately on His return from the wilderness Jesus was walking by the Sea of Galilee and saw two brothers, Peter and Andrew, who were fishermen.

And he said unto them, "Follow me and I will make you fishers of men".
(Matthew 4:19)

Just as the evil one feared, Jesus was starting to recruit soldiers for His army. The first two selected as disciples were Peter and Andrew. These men appeared to be hand-picked, and not from among the ranks of the priests with whom Satan had an existing alliance. They were the "salt of the earth", simple fishermen who were not contaminated with the doctrine (or leaven) of the Pharisees, ideal raw material for the Lion to mold into spiritual commandos.

Most corporate executives advising Jesus on strategy, would have suggested that He at least speak with the priests and religious rulers, to see if He could win them over to His side. After all, they were God's representatives to the Jewish people, they knew the scripture which Jesus had now fashioned into a sword, and would probably be easier to bring up to speed on His agenda. With the exception of Nicodemus whose heart was different, Jesus did not attempt to woo the chief priests.

Jesus did not come to earth on a goodwill tour or to play politics. So rather than go *to* them, He went *after* them...with His sword. Jesus was intent on knocking over the building blocks that the devil used to keep man in darkness, including the arrogance and hypocrisy that had infected the Jewish clergy.

Jesus' recruitment strategy for His new army was very well considered. He avoided those who were righteous in their own eyes and selected simple men, like James and John, who could exercise simple faith and learn to walk humbly in obedience. These are still the requirements to enlist in His army today, simple faith and humble obedience. Jesus continues to carefully select disciples (including Judas who betrayed Him) and they all leave their normal lives and follow after Him. Like a man sitting in a dentist's chair, Satan looked on, nervously anticipating what was to come.

He did not have long to wait. Immediately after selecting James and John, the Lion launches another blistering attack on the kingdom of darkness. He begins in Galilee (Matthew 4:23), spreading dangerous ideas about how man can have a relationship with God (preaching the gospel of the kingdom) and then, goes through Syria (Matthew 4:24), healing sicknesses, curing diseases and casting out devils. The kingdom of darkness is in chaos and turmoil!

The Lion establishes His authority over unclean spirits and begins casting them out of the human hosts that they inhabited for years. This is unprecedented in the history of man. Everywhere Jesus goes, the story is the same. He teaches the people, heals the sick and casts out devils. The more He does this, the bigger the crowd becomes, first by fifties, then by hundreds, and then by many thousands. The satanic world is now operating in panic mode. Satan was finding it difficult to maintain order and control over his legions. Principalities and powers were in an uproar. They were all very afraid of this Jesus and of the authority He exercised over them.

> When evening had come, they brought unto Him many who were demon-possessed. And he cast out the spirits with His word and healed all who were sick.
> (Matthew 8:16).

So afraid were Satan's demons of the Lion that as soon as

they saw Him coming, they would tremble (James 2:19) and beg Him not to hurt them.

> And he cried out with a loud voice, and said, "What have I to do with You, Jesus, Son of the Most High God? I implore You by God, that You do not torment me." For He said unto him, "Come out of the man, unclean spirit!" Then He asked him, "What is your name?" And he answered saying, "My name is Legion for we are many."
> (Mark 5:7-9)

Unclean spirits of every rank, from the lowest to the devil himself, all recognized who Jesus was and the power that He held over them. They were truly afraid of Him. Jesus' plan of attack was simple. Go into densely populated areas, major cities, towns and synagogues and destroy the work of the devil wherever He found it.

But as bad as this was for Satan, it was going to get much worse. The Lion was about to turn up the heat on the dragon.

> And when He had called His twelve disciples to Him, He gave them power over unclean spirits, to cast them out and to heal all kinds of sickness and all kinds of disease.
> (Matthew 10:1)

Satan's long-standing, deep-rooted fear, which goes back to his concern when Adam was created, is that man would develop spiritual authority and exercise dominion over him. **This is exactly where the Lion was taking this battle,** empower ordinary men to cast out unclean spirits and destroy the very fiber of the devil's kingdom. Satan had no answer to this. Jesus' disciples were invading his territory, casting out his devils, ripping his whole world apart.

Demons who were once in control of man, were now

subject to their authority in Jesus' name. They were in a state of panic and looking to their leader for a solution. In one such incident, the disciples encountered a very strong demon that had taken control of a man. The disciples tried to cast the spirit out without any success. Jesus had to intervene and cast the demon out Himself. We pick up the account from Matthew 9:28

> And when He had come into the house, His disciples asked him privately, "Why could not we cast it out?" And He said unto them, "This kind can come out by nothing but prayer and fasting."
> (Mark 9:28-29)

The disciples were puzzled. We have cast out demons before, why couldn't we get this one to leave? Jesus used the opportunity to give His disciples their first lesson in advanced commando training, how to recognize different demonic entities and ranks (*"this kind"*) and how to breakdown the enemy's strongholds in combat (*by "prayer and fasting"*). He was teaching His recruits **spiritual warfare!** This could not be good news for the devil and his now terrified underlings.

But it gets worse for Satan.

Within a very short space of time, the Lion intensifies the pressure by sending out this time, not twelve, but seventy of his followers into the cities to cast out devils and heal the sick.

> Then the seventy returned with joy, saying, "Lord, even the devils are subject unto us in Your name".
> (Luke 10:17)

Where was this going to end? At this rate, pretty soon there would be more men with power over demons, than there were demons on the earth. Satan could only watch on helplessly as his evil empire crumbled around him. If he did not do something soon, there would be no kingdom of darkness to rule. He knew now, that he now had no choice. *Strike the shepherd and the sheep will scatter* (Matthew 26:31).

While the Lion was intensifying His assault on the kingdom of darkness, He was, at the same time exposing the hypocrisy and false doctrine of the Jewish clergy. Over the years, they had become more aligned with the purposes of the devil, than with God whom they claimed to serve. Here is Jesus' scathing indictment of them:

"But woe unto you scribes and Pharisees, hypocrites! For you shut up the kingdom of heaven against men; for you neither go in yourselves, nor do you allow those who are entering to go in. Woe unto you scribes and Pharisees, hypocrites! For you devour widows' houses, and for a pretense make long prayers. Therefore ye shall receive the greater damnation."
(Matthew 23:13-14)

Jesus was not afraid to expose the corruption in the religious system of His day and to make an open shame of those who used God's grace to lord it over others. This was His position then and it continues to be His position in the church today.

(*Note to self*: If God ever appoints me to any position of responsibility in His church, I better make sure that I serve Him humbly and in good faith).

Jesus' constant exposure of the moral corruption and

spiritual ignorance of the priests, caused them to hate Him, to the point of wanting Him dead. The more Jesus put them to public shame, the more the devil fanned their anger and resentment. Satan saw the Jewish priests as the instrument that he would eventually use to kill the Lion and he wanted them primed for the occasion.

However, while the priests hated Jesus, they feared the people who counted Him as a prophet. Satan was under pressure to do something about the Lion before He destroyed his kingdom and these indecisive priests were simply not moving quickly enough.

In what I believe to be a moment of blind panic, Satan steps out of the shadows and gets directly and personally involved in the plot to kill Jesus. He was forced by Jesus' relentless attacks to take immediate action. Jesus had to be stopped, and left to these indecisive, incompetent priests, this was going to take another month, maybe two. Satan couldn't wait that long. As we saw earlier, Satan enters Judas, Jesus is betrayed, condemned and executed by crucifixion. As predicted, when the shepherd was struck down, all the sheep scattered. Every one of His disciples ran and hid when Jesus was captured. Men, who weeks before were exercising authority over demons, and claiming that they would die for Him, were now afraid to say that they were once a part of the Lion's army. Some followed from a distance while the Lion was first beaten and then nailed to a cross. Although Jesus told them this was going to happen, those who were once so excited about being with Him, were now devastated that the work that He started had come to an end. Those who could, went back to fishing, while a small remnant stayed close, consoling and supporting each other in this time of grief.

This would seem a very strange end for the Lion.

Everything He did up until now seemed strategically brilliant. How could He allow himself to be silenced so easily? Instead of rallying His troops and fighting to prevent his own death, He seemed willing to go to the cross. Why would He allow Satan to put an end to all that He had accomplished over the last three years? Why give up without a fight?

This was God's plan from the foundation of the world.

I believe that Jesus' intensified pressure on the kingdom of darkness was deliberate and its intent was to force Satan to take the lead in the plot to kill Him. Jesus came to the earth to die. His mission was to take upon Himself the sin of the world and be crucified in man's place. Jesus is the *"Lamb that was slain from the foundation of the world"* (Revelation 13:8). God had been planning this from the very beginning.

But the brilliance of God's eternal plan is this. Not only did the shedding of Jesus' blood release man from the consequences of sin, the pressure applied by the Lion, which drove Satan to carry out the act, was the cause of the devil's downfall. The crucifixion of the Christ not only saved the world, it caused Satan to condemn himself.

Exactly how this was achieved, and the implications for us today, we will see next, as we consider "The slaying of the dragon".

CHAPTER 9

THE SLAYING OF THE DRAGON

The crucifixion of Jesus is the most significant event in God's strategic plan and by extension, man's existence on the earth. This is the focal point of all history. Before Christ everything looked forward and pointed to the Messiah who was to come. Since then, time looks back to and is counted from His presence on earth.

Jesus' death is the key to God's strategic plan because of what it accomplished for man. Everything else in His life, being born of a virgin, the miracles He performed, the words He spoke, would have all been in vain, if He did not die and come out of the grave. Paul in writing to the Corinthians said:

> And if Christ is not risen, then our preaching is empty and your faith is also empty.
> (1 Corinthians 15:14)

There are many people today, who believe and accept that Jesus lived on the earth two thousand years ago and that He was a "good man" or a "great teacher". It is true that all of His words point man towards living a moral, responsible, honest, Godly life. But if this is all that Jesus means to us, then, like the Jews of His day, we have entirely missed the point.

I have wondered what it would be like to be alive during Jesus' time on the earth, to hear Him speak and see the miracles that He did. *Would I have recognized Him as the Son of God?* To a very large extent, we today have a far better view of who Jesus is than the people of His day. Yes they got to hear Him speak, and were astounded as He healed the sick and raised the dead, but very few of them recognized Him for who He was, and is. In fact, although He told them time and time again, none of His disciples truly understood that His primary purpose in coming to earth was to die. Here are some of His conversations with them:

> "Therefore My Father loves Me, because I lay down My life that I may take it again. No one takes it from Me, but I lay it down of Myself. I have power to lay it down and I have power to take it again..."
> (John 10: 17-18).

> For He taught His disciples and said unto them, "The Son of Man is being betrayed into the hands of men, and they will kill Him. And after He is killed, He will rise the third day"
> (Mark 9:31).

> "just as the Son of Man did not come to be served, but to serve and to give His life a ransom for many"
> (Matthew 20:28).

Jesus came to lay down His life and offer Himself a ransom for us. His death is the strategic key that unlocked the power of God to save mankind. Since this is so, it would appear that Satan unknowingly played into God's hands (so to speak) by orchestrating the capture and execution of

Jesus. Here is what the Apostle Paul had to say about this:

> But we speak the wisdom of God in a mystery, the hidden wisdom which God ordained before the ages for our glory, which none of the rulers of this age knew; for if they had known, they would not have crucified the Lord of glory.
> (1 Corinthians 2:7-8)

In verse 7, Paul confirms that God had a secret agenda, a **"hidden wisdom"**, which He orchestrated and put into place on our behalf, before the world began. This is in fact, what we had set out to investigate at the start of our review. Our opening question was "Is there a hidden plan in scripture that involves man and points back to God?" Paul confirms that all of these things are in fact so.

But even further, in verse 8, Paul confirms that God's strategy was so superior and so well disguised ("the hidden wisdom"), that no one in the devil's camp (the rulers of this age) recognized it, because if they did, *they would never have crucified Christ.*

So what was God's secret strategy and how did He use Satan to achieve it? From the very beginning, God had two pressing problems to address: How to redeem man from sin and how to destroy the kingdom of darkness that Satan had established on the earth. According to divine order, the only means of remission for sin, was the shedding of sinless blood. But no one on the earth, qualified as sinless. Man was sinful and couldn't save himself.

The only person who qualified as sinless was God Himself, so God came in the form of a man to be that sacrifice. To be the propitiation for our sins, the savior could not come to earth, live a sinless life *and then die of old age, or natural causes.* His blood had to be shed for the curse of sin to be broken.

This is where the devil came into God's plan. Jesus in John 8:44 said that Satan was "a murderer from the beginning". In his hatred for God and man, he would not hesitate to take anyone's life, if it would advance or protect his kingdom. Satan's unwitting role in God's strategic plan was the part he played in the killing of the Son of God.

How to slay a dragon:

Satan was the author of his own destruction. Jesus' assault on the kingdom of darkness, caused such fear in the spirit realm, that it prompted the devil to play a direct role in a murder plot. I submit that this is the first time in recorded history, that Satan is positively identified as playing a personal and direct role in the killing of a human being.

Even in the killing of Job's children, scripture said "a great wind from the wilderness" struck the house, (which modern insurance companies erroneously call "an act of God") and it fell on them. Although we are certain that this was Satan's doing, the evidence is circumstantial. All the other murders in the world, were committed by humans, who were driven by their own lusts to act.

Remember what James said about how sin grows from thought to act:

> But each one is tempted when he is drawn away by his own desires and enticed.
> (James 1:14)

We are tempted, or encouraged to sin, by yielding to our own desires or "lusts". Take, for example, the case against Herod, King of Judea. Herod committed one of the most unforgivable crimes known to man, the slaughter of innocent babies. But why did he do it? Herod was drawn away from normal moral thinking by his lust to protect his own political future, and his indignation that someone claiming to be king should arise in his domain.

This is the lust for power that motivates men even today. That is what drove Herod. Yes, the idea to order the killings would have come from Satan, but the lust that drove Herod to act was his own. Even though Herod's action was influenced by Satan, the one defense that he cannot make when he stands before God to account for killing these children, is "The devil made me do it". His lust for power made him do it. And that has been the pattern of sin through the ages.

The one justification that Adam could not use as a defense for eating the fruit is, "Eve made me do it". Similarly, Eve could not excuse herself by saying, "The serpent made me do it". The one defense that you and I cannot rely on is, "The devil made me do it". It appears that any attempt to blame Satan for our sin will be a hard sell in the court of heaven.

So, what exactly is the devil guilty of? What did he do to deserve judgment? Well, he rebelled against God. OK, but he was also expelled from heaven. He attacked Job, a righteous man. Yes but that was endorsed by God. He has tormented man and deceived the whole world (Revelation 12:9). Yes, but that is a consequence of man's sin.

Where is the "smoking gun" in the devil's hand?

I submit that the "smoking gun" is in the personal role he played in Jesus' death. The standard of evidence established in the court of heaven is:

> Whoever is deserving of death shall be put to death on the testimony of two or three witnesses;

(Deuteronomy 17:6)

So, here are your two witnesses:

> Then Satan entered Judas surnamed Iscariot who was
> numbered among the twelve
> (Luke 22:3)

> Now after the piece of bread, Satan entered into him. Then
> Jesus said unto him, "What you do, do quickly."
> (John 13:27)

These two verses of scripture positively identify Satan as entering into Judas and acting through him to betray Jesus. This is different from the process of temptation explained in James above. The devil did not stay on the outside and dangle the thirty pieces of silver in front of Judas to entice him. By the time Judas approached the priests to discuss a price, Satan had already entered into and was in full possession of him. Satan was able to commandeer Judas because he made himself an easy target for evil.

But did Satan actually kill Jesus? From what scripture says, apparently not. It was in fact the chief priests and the Romans who actually condemned and crucified Jesus. Satan in Judas, was the betrayer, the one who instigated it and therefore just as guilty as if he committed the act personally. Satan was the instigator in the death of an innocent man. But how do we establish that Jesus was in fact innocent? Let us examine the transcript from His public trial:

> Jesus saith unto him, "It is as you said. Nevertheless I say to
> you hereafter you will see the Son of Man sitting on the
> right hand of the Power, and coming on the clouds of
> heaven." Then the high priest tore his clothes saying, "He
> hath spoken blasphemy! What further need do we have of

witnesses? Look now you have heard his blasphemy!"
(Matthew 26:64-65)

The charge against Jesus was blasphemy, or the offense of great disrespect or profanity against God. When Jesus was brought before the chief priest, He was asked to explain whom He was. Jesus spoke truthfully and identified Himself as God on earth and the right hand of power in heaven. To the priest, a man making himself equal with God was the vilest and most offensive form of blasphemy for which there could be only one punishment:

> "And whoever blasphemes the name of the Lord shall surely be put to death."
> (Leviticus 24:16)

But Jesus was not guilty of blasphemy because He spoke the truth about who He was and so was innocent of the crime for which He was charged. In fact, Jesus' innocence goes beyond the crime of blasphemy laid against Him. He was also innocent of the charge of sin. 1Corinthians 5:21 says that Jesus *knew no sin* but became sin for us. Jesus was therefore an innocent man and blameless according to the spirit and the letter of the law.

The chief priest did not recognize Jesus as the Son of God:

> He was in the world, and the world was made through Him and the world did not know Him. He came unto His own and His own did not receive Him.
> (John 1:10-11)

So, as far as they concerned, they were *legally crucifying a proven blasphemer* (this will not excuse them).

Likewise, the Roman soldiers who whipped Jesus and nailed Him to the cross were hard, cruel men executing someone found guilty by a competent court and sentenced to death. They certainly did not know who this Man really was. As a matter of fact, Jesus was one of three "convicted criminals" executed that day.

The only person who recognized Jesus as the innocent Son of God, was Satan. In fact the entire demonic host knew that Jesus was the Son of God:

> And the unclean spirits, whenever they saw Him, fell down before Him and cried out, saying, "You are the Son of God."
> (Mark 3:11)

They knew who He was, knew He was innocent and yet they delivered Him to be executed. Carrying out this act in spite of this knowledge, makes Satan guilty of directly betraying innocent blood. God's word is the standard by which all things will be judged. Even God has subjected Himself to His own word.

> For You have magnified Your word above Your name.
> (Psalm 138:2)

So what does God's word say about this particular crime?

> "Cursed is the one who takes a bribe to slay an innocent person. And all the people said Amen!"
> (Deuteronomy 27:25)

Satan entered into Judas, who then took a bribe to betray an innocent man to be put to death. But wait a minute, the curse is on "the one who takes a bribe"; Satan did not take the bribe, Judas did.

Not so fast.

Scripture clearly establishes the principle of vicarious action. Paul, in explaining to the Jews the Lordship of Jesus over the priestly order, indicated that Levi paid tithes to Melchizedek before he was born, while still in Abraham's loins.

> Even Levi, who receives tithes, paid tithes through Abraham, so to speak, for he was still in the loins of his father when Melchizedek met him.
> (Hebrews 7:9-10)

Even though Levi did not personally pay tithes to Melchizedek, he did so vicariously as Abraham's descendant. So too, while Satan did not physically collect the thirty pieces of silver, he did so vicariously while in possession of Judas. As a result, he is as guilty as Judas was of taking a bribe to slay an innocent person, and therefore brought himself under the condemnation and curse of the law.

Gotcha!

This was what I believe God was carefully crafting in His strategic plan, using the pages of Scripture to photograph the elusive devil with a smoking gun in his hand. This is every prosecutor's dream come true. Live video of the accused committing the crime. When Satan is judged, at the top of the list of all his evils will be this one. In fact, all those who played a part in Jesus' crucifixion will have to answer for it. Standing at the front of the line, will be Judas, Satan and his demonic host. Jesus said, *"but woe to that man by whom the Son of man is betrayed"* (Mark 14:21).The case against them is ironclad.

This is the point that Paul was making:

Which none of the rulers of this age knew: for if they had known it, they would not have crucified the Lord of glory. (1 Corinthians 2:8)

According to Paul, if Satan knew that by crucifying Jesus he was placing himself in jeopardy twice, by first providing the means to redeem man, and at the same time taking the curse of the law upon himself, he would never have done so. This was God's secret agenda. God no longer has to condemn Satan, Satan has condemned himself by instigating the death of an innocent man and is cursed under the law.

The perfect strategic plan:
Here is what I consider to be the beauty of God's Strategic Plan. Do you remember the renowned military general Sun Tzu whom we mentioned in the first chapter? As we said, General Tzu's strategies are studied even today for insights into modern business decision making. Here is one of his most famous quotes:

"The supreme art of war is to subdue the enemy without fighting".

This is exactly what God did. He didn't condemn Satan; He positioned him to condemn himself. That according to General Tzu, is the supreme art of war. There are no words that can adequately describe God's strategic plan of salvation. "Brilliant" just doesn't do it justice. God, in one supremely divine move, has solved forever the problem of having to judge Satan.

> For if God did not spare the angels who sinned, but cast them down to hell and delivered them into chains of darkness to be reserved unto judgment...
> (2 Peter 2:4)

Wait, but there is more. *There is a divine irony to all this.*

Remember what Satan desired first and foremost? To sit on the Throne. The lust that started all of this was the desire to be like the most High. This is what led to the rebellion in heaven and how Lucifer became Satan. The irony is that the very man whom Satan despised and hated, has, *in Christ,* been elevated to exactly that position.

> But God who is rich in mercy, because of His great love with which He loved us, even when we were dead in trespasses, made us alive together with Christ (by grace you have been saved) and has raised us up together in heavenly places in Christ Jesus."
> (Ephesians 2:6)

The King James Version says "raised us up together *and made us sit together* in heavenly places in Christ Jesus" (Emphasis added). Jesus told the scribes at his trial that they would one day see Him sit at the right hand of Power in heaven. Apparently as the Bride of Christ, the Church will too. Not only is redeemed man elevated to heavenly places in Christ, but he will also have spiritual authority over angelic beings. Paul, in writing to the Corinthians, said:

> Do you not know that we shall judge angels? How much more things that pertain to this life?
> (1 Corinthians 6:3)

God's divine, strategic genius is that, not only has He allowed Satan to condemn himself, but through the Blood of the Lamb He has elevated lowly, insignificant, undeserving, puny, wretched man, **to sit in the very place that Satan wanted for himself.**

Satan knows this now and it will be a part of his eternal torment. This is a fitting outcome for the evil one and it certainly was not what he anticipated when he orchestrated the plot to kill Jesus.

Our next chapters take us to the conclusion of God's great strategic plan, where we see the restoration of man to a position of spiritual authority and the great destiny that God has created for us all.

CHAPTER 10

THE TRIUMPH OF THE LAMB

It is now apparent that scripture does contain a coherent, deliberate strategic plan to achieve a specific long term objective. This plan which took thousands of years to come to fruition, is focused on two real world issues, destroying evil and freeing slaves. We saw how Jesus, as the conquering Lion of the Tribe of Judah, defeated man's and God's eternal enemy, in an unprecedented demonstration of spiritual power and might.

Now we will consider what this same Jesus, through His selfless sacrifice as the Lamb of God has done to save man from eternal judgment and free him from living in bondage. Before we go on to examine the benefits of Jesus' sacrifice for us, the question we must ask ourselves is whether God's plan which was documented thousands of years ago, is still relevant and applicable to us in modern times.

In general, strategic plans are written for a relevant period of time or a "planning horizon". In a business context, this is the length of time that a company would consider appropriate for making future projections, usually no more than 5 years. Every student of business strategy knows that it is important to review, update and revise your plan as time goes by, to ensure that it continues to be relevant and applicable to changing circumstances.

God's Strategic Plan, however, remains the same unchanged since the moment that Jesus said *"It is finished"*, and died on the cross. A valid question would be "How could what He did then, be relevant to us *now*?" In this rapidly changing environment and in the face of all of the uncertainty that there is in the world, how could a two thousand year old plan *for anything* be still relevant today?

Our society is so much more advanced today, than it was back when Jesus walked on the earth. Science and technology have improved our standard of living, to an extent that would be thought impossible back then. New discoveries and developments in the fields of medicine, communications, engineering, food production, transportation, weaponry, and so many others, are impacting the way we live, almost on a daily basis. As a result, belief in a Savior who lived and died two thousand years ago is considered so old fashioned by many today. How could anything that He did, or said, back then have any bearing on us today?

The answer to our question is that, although modern society is now highly developed and man is very advanced in many respects, *his heart has remained the same as it always was.* **God's strategic plan addresses issues of man's heart, not his head.**

Man is still plagued by sin, jealousy, anger, lust, insecurities, depression, greed, hatred, intolerance, impure motives, addictions and the whole host of sin-related issues, which affect us today, in the same way that it did our ancestors.

God's plan for man, remains fresh and relevant in every generation, because science has not yet, nor will it ever, develop a cure for sin. The biggest problem in the world today, is not a lack of technology to provide us with greater comfort, but sin, which leads to selfishness, injustice and crime at a personal level and in the wider community. This in turn produces the social, economic and political issues that get reported daily in the news. So while we may be much more accomplished now, man's heart hasn't changed a bit since the day that Adam first sinned. To fully appreciate this, let us go back in time and examine the condition of man's heart in Old Testament days to see if there is any difference between then and now.

God led the Jews out of slavery in Egypt (Exodus 15) and brought them to a place where He could mold them into a people of His own. While they were under the whip in Egypt, they had no freedom of choice and were forced to do as they were told. Now that they were free to make their own decisions, God introduced the law, so that they could know how to maintain good relations with Him (Exodus 20:1-11) and with each other (Exodus 20:12-17).

The basic human-relations premise of God's law is, as Jesus said, to "do unto others as you would have them do unto you" (Luke 6:31). You don't want anyone stealing from you, so don't steal from others; you don't want anyone attacking and killing you, then don't commit murder; you don't like to be deceived, then be truthful and honest in your dealings with others. In order to maintain law and order among the Israelites, God appointed judges, kings and priests to lead, direct and govern them in accordance with His laws and commandments. Let's see how this worked out.

In 1 Kings 3:16, we are told of two women who appear before the court of King Solomon, each claiming to be the mother of a particular child. The child obviously couldn't speak for himself and probably resembled both women. There was no natural way to tell whose baby this was.

Solomon, acting under the wisdom of God, introduces Old Testament DNA testing to Israel. His decision was to cut the baby in half and give each woman her share. The real mother is distraught and would rather give up her self-interest of keeping the child so that it could live. The other woman doesn't care about the child, *she wants what she wants* and since her baby is dead, she has no problem in letting Solomon cut the other woman's baby in half.

This is the human condition, yesterday, today and forever. **We want what we want**, even if someone else has to suffer. This, expressed in modern vernacular is, "The heart wants what the heart wants" (2001, Woody Allen, quoting Emily Dickinson, to justify his affair with Mia Farrow's adopted daughter). We want what we want and every one else just has to "deal with it".**This is the root cause of all sin, big and small**.

What makes government and our legal system as necessary in today's world as it was back in Old Testament times, *is man's selfishness in action.* People talk about electing government officials who would seek the "best interests of the country". The problem is that, the perception of "the best interest of the country" can vary radically from person to person because our individual interests differ. What we really mean is that we want a government that will seek our interests, even if that conflicts with the interests of others. Today's world of fiscal cliffs and government shut downs takes us all the way back to Solomon and the baby. Our government grapples with the same underlying issues now, as Solomon did back then.

The irony is that we pat ourselves on the back, because we are part of "civilized society". But remove the police service, the military and all law enforcement and you will see sin in our society like never before. We will regress back to the days of the "wild, wild west", or more likely Sodom and Gomorrah in no time at all. This is what the so-called "doomsday preppers" predict will happen, some time in the future. Their premise is that, one day, something catastrophic will occur in society, law and order will break down and man's sinful nature will be unleashed. They are arming themselves and stockpiling supplies, just in case.

This is how God sums up the human condition:

> For the heart *(of man)* is deceitful above all things and desperately wicked: who can know it?
> (Jeremiah 17:9), (Emphasis added).

We are forced to conclude that modern man is no different in nature from our ancestors. If anything, we have become more of a danger to ourselves and sin is still the underlying issue in our lives. *God's strategic plan is even more relevant and badly needed today than ever before.*

In addition to the issue of sin, we are just as unsure of the meaning of life today as man has ever been. It seems that as technology makes the world smaller, the pace of life becomes faster and many people are locked in a process of burning the candle at both ends, just to survive. Have you ever asked yourself any of these questions:

- Where is my life heading?

- Why do I feel so empty inside?

- Is there a purpose to my life?

- How do I get out of this rut that I find myself in?

Some of our lives are really messed up. Modern society

glamorizes the lifestyle of the rich and famous, and many of their fans and followers looking on from the outside, long for what they have. Sadly, many of us are following an empty dream, hoping to achieve fame, fortune, popularity, and the respect and admiration of the world.

Unfortunately, many have had their souls "pierced through with many sorrows" (1 Timothy 6:10), as they find, after achieving all that they set out to, that riches and glamor are not the same as contentment, joy, and peace. It seems that excessive, self-indulgent behavior, often accompanies success and fame, because deep down, our soul can never really be satisfied by an abundance of things.

Jesus Himself warned of this modern day paradox which I call "discontent in the face of plenty".

> And He said unto them, "Take heed and beware of covetousness, for one's life does not consist in the abundance of the things he possesses."
> (Luke 12:15)

Sure, our lives would be much more comfortable if we were all rich, but that does not mean we would be happy and contented. There are many people today who are living in the lap of luxury, but they are unhappy, bitter, angry and depressed. Why? **Because money may gratify the flesh, but it cannot feed the soul.**

Even ordinary, "regular" people, living ordinary regular lives, can get trapped in the rat race. Product vendors tell us that our lives would be so much improved if we owned that new car, took that luxurious vacation, or bought the latest gadget. We fall for the hype and mortgage our futures to afford the things we think will make us happy. We soon realize, that although "things" can't satisfy our souls, they can cause us stress, as we max-out our credit cards.

While some of us are trapped in the rat race, others are locked in a prison without walls. Some people go through "dark" periods in their lives, because something bad happens, which causes them to lose hope. The loss of a job; of a loved one; of financial security, are real emotional hazards in today's world. People who lose hope are candidates for anxiety, depression, anger, violent outbursts and sometimes become abusive to themselves or to those that they love. There is no doubt this world that we live in can wear us down and break our spirits, which is why God's strategic plan and the benefits secured by the Lamb are of such vital importance to us *right now.*

What are the benefits of God's plan?

One of the very first things that Jesus did, at the start of His ministry, was to announce to the world, the benefits we would derive from His sacrifice:

> "The Spirit of the Lord is upon Me, because He hath anointed Me to preach the gospel to the poor; He has sent Me to heal the brokenhearted, to proclaim liberty to the captives and recovering of sight to the blind, to set at liberty those who are oppressed; to proclaim the acceptable year of the Lord".
> (Luke 4:18-19)

This declaration, made in a synagogue in Jesus' home-town of Nazareth, is a summary of all that God has provided for us through Jesus. God has anointed (or empowered) Him to:

1) Preach the gospel (or "good news") to the poor.
Notice that Jesus did not say that he came to eradicate poverty in the earth. Many people, mostly the poor,

followed Jesus around from city to city, not because He made them rich, but because He gave them hope. People lose hope when they feel that they have no way out of a bad situation. This could apply to the poor and to the wealthy alike. The human spirit needs hope to survive. When we lose hope, we lose our reason to go on and the world can become a very dark place.

The best cure for hopelessness is good news. That is what Jesus came to provide, not a false hope based on empty promises, but hope based on the certainty, that as we put our trust in Him, He will never leave us nor forsake us. Jesus came to give rich and poor the good news that there is an eternal hope, which He offers to all men:

> "Let not your heart be troubled; you believe in God, believe also in Me. In My Father's house are many mansions; if it were not so, I would have told you. I go to prepare a place for you. And if I go and prepare a place for you, I will come again and receive you to Myself; that where I am there you may be also."
> (John 14:1-3)

The hope that Jesus offers, is that as we put our trust in Him, *He* will work things out in our lives, no matter how dark they may seem at the moment. These are not empty words. What we realize is that as we let go of ourselves and put our trust in Him, those fears, insecurities and deep seated anxieties that sometimes control our lives, are replaced with a sense of peace, assurance and hope that is impossible to explain to the outside world.

> And we know that all things work together for good to those who love God, to those who are the called according to His purpose.
> (Romans 8:28)

God works all things, the good, the bad and the ugly, to our ultimate benefit when we put our faith in Him. No the birds don't always sing and the deer don't always feed from our hands, but we have this confidence that through all of life's experiences, He is right there with us working on our behalf. You can't get any better source of hope than that.

2) Heal the brokenhearted.

People who live without hope for too long can sometimes become so dysfunctional that not even good news can lift them up. When we are brokenhearted, not only do we lose hope we lose the ability to function normally. When our physical hearts no longer function, we die physically. So it is in the spirit. There are many of us walking around in a spiritual daze, alive on the outside but dead on the inside. We are unable to build healthy relationships, to escape the feeling of gloom, to positively impact the lives of other people.

In my personal experience, a broken heart is the result of either emotional or psychological trauma suffered either as adults or when we were children, or a lifestyle of sin that opens us up to spiritual depression. In either case, God needs to fix our hearts, or more appropriately, give us a new heart, so we can live again. If this is you, then Jesus came to give you a new heart and a new spirit.

Create in me a clean heart, O God, and renew a steadfast spirit within me. Do not cast me away from Your presence and do not take Your Holy Spirit from me. Restore unto me the joy of Your salvation and uphold me by Your generous Spirit.
(Psalm 51:10-11)

King David, who penned these words, had fallen into a very deep pit in his life. He abused his power as God's anointed king over Israel, had a man killed and took his wife as his own. In response, God sent His prophet Nathan to confront David. When David came to his senses and realized the horror of what he had done, rather than blame the woman as Adam did, or hide from God, he reached out to God and appealed, not just for forgiveness for what he had done, but for an intervention in his life. "Please God, create in me a clean heart".

This is what Jesus came to do for us, heal our broken-heartedness by changing our lives.

The sacrifice of the Lamb has already made this benefit available to us all, but, like David, we must reach out to God to access His grace. It's like having a medical emergency. A person in cardiac arrest has to get to the hospital for the doctors to save him or her. The facility is already there, but we must reach out and access it.

Sometimes our hearts become so broken, that we are immobilized and paralyzed spiritually and unable to reach out to God. This is why He would often send someone, like He sent Nathan to David, to reach out to us. God didn't send Nathan the prophet to chastise or condemn David, but to reach out to him and help him, by forcing him to acknowledge his sin. This is the first step in getting out of the pit that we find ourselves in.

If your heart is broken and God has sent someone to reach out to you, don't shrink away. Pray as Peter did, "Lord help me", and reach back. If no one has reached out to you (other than me in this note), then find someone who knows the Lord and who you can trust and let him or her know you need help.

Or, if you prefer, you can go to God yourself and ask Him to heal your broken heart. Psalm 51 is, in my opinion, the most potent medicine we can ever have to help us recover from spiritual trauma. It sets out in detail how David was able to get up, after an almost fatal spiritual fall. Read through this Psalm, let it speak to you, make it your own prayer and reach back out to the Lord. He will not turn away anyone who comes to Him with a broken heart.

3) Proclaim liberty to the captives:

Jesus came to deliver man from slavery *to* sin and to free us from being bruised *by* sin. Slavery of all types imposes two forms of evil on man: captivity and brutality. Sin does not just enslave us; it takes a toll on our lives by inflicting brutal punishment on us. Sin is the ultimate narcotic. We have all seen, or heard of cases of young people, who got hooked on heroin, "meth" or cocaine.

As the drug is injected into their bloodstream, they experience a high that is indescribable. That high puts them into a state of stupor, to the extent that they are not aware of anything else happening around them. As soon as the high evaporates, the addictive nature of the drug drives them to do whatever they must, to get more to achieve the same high.

After doing this repeatedly for a period of days, months and years, the radiant child that every one knew and loved disappears, and is replaced by an addict who is physically and emotionally devastated by the drug. Such is the effect of sin in our lives. It is just not as visible to everyone else. Sin feels good because it gratifies our flesh, but it is brutal on our minds, our emotions and even our bodies. Sin is addictive. The more we practise sin the more it takes a hold on us.

> Jesus answered them, "Most assuredly, I say to you, whoever commits sin is a slave of sin. And the slave does not abide in the house for ever, but a son abides forever. Therefore if the Son makes you free, you shall be free indeed."
> (John 8:34-36)

Jesus explained the effect of sin and bondage on our lives. In verse 34 He said, "anyone who commits sin is the slave of sin". This applies to all of us, we are enslaved by sin. But He continued, "but if I set you free, you are free for sure". *Free for sure*, but how? How does this work in practice, *in my life*? Jesus explains the process of becoming free in John chapter 8:

> Then said Jesus to those Jews who believed Him, "If you abide in my word, you are my disciples indeed. And you shall know the truth and the truth shall make you free."
> (John 8:31-32)

This passage of scripture, is in my opinion, the most powerful and potent scripture reference for us to grasp, because it sets out the process by which we are set free from sin. Notice that Jesus spoke these words not to the Pharisees, nor to the world at large, but to those Jews *who believed Him*. The first point is that for Jesus to be our deliverer, we have to believe (put our whole trust and confidence) in Him. After we take this initial step here is what happens next:

If we abide or continue is His word.
We have to continuously attend to God's word, study it, meditate on it, let it permeate our hearts, and act on it (be doers, not just readers). We will see that Jesus' word is the active ingredient in transforming our lives. "The words that

I speak to you", Jesus said, "they are spirit and they are life" (John 6:63). To become free, we have to first make God's word a priority in our lives.

Then we will become His disciples indeed.
Discipleship, or becoming like Jesus, is an important part of becoming free. The mechanics of God's strategic plan, is to create free men and women, using Jesus as our prototype or example. This is how God frees us. When Adam sinned, death passed to all men because we inherited Adam's "human" or sin nature. God's brilliant strategy, is to free man from sin, by having us take on the nature and character of Jesus, who was Himself *sinless*. Freedom from sin involves an exchange of Adam's nature for Jesus' nature as we become His disciples.

We will know the truth
There are two elements of knowing "the truth" that we experience as we come into contact with God's word. First, comes the life changing realization that we have been set free. Calvary was in effect God's Emancipation Proclamation for all men, that Jesus' sacrifice has paid the final price to set us free from sin.

The problem is that, until we become aware of the provision of this freedom (through the truth of the Gospel), we continue to live indifferent to God and slaves to sin. When the truth of God's salvation penetrates our hearts, our lives are changed. Almost in an instant, we realize that this is all real; God is real; His love is real; eternity is real. This "knowing" causes us to surrender our lives to the strategic God who orchestrated this all for our benefit. This initial surrender is the first aspect of really knowing the truth and it results in us being translated from the kingdom of darkness into the Kingdom of God's dear Son. There however a second aspect of knowing the truth which goes beyond the act of *setting* us free, to drive the process of *making* us free.

*And the truth shall **make you free***

Man was set free in one act on Calvary and as we accept this truth as a personal conviction, God's salvation takes instant effect in our lives. Our hearts change and we experience a connection and closeness to God like we have never felt before. God is no longer a "force of the universe" or character in a book, but a real Person who establishes a personal relationship with us. This is what Jesus referred to as being "born-again" in John 3:3.

But this is just the beginning of what God wants to achieve in our lives. After we have been set free, comes the process of being *made free* or learning how to walk in freedom. The act of setting a bird free involves first opening the door to its cage. There are some birds that have lived in their cages for so long that even after you open the door, they will not fly away. They have become institutionalized by their cages.

Many of us have lived shackled to sin for so long, that even though we have been set free and have a personal relationship with God, we continue to function as if we are still in bondage. We have become institutionalized by sin. This is why Jesus wants us to abide or live in His word. The truth of God's word is the active ingredient in the process of making us free, by showing us how to live, no longer as servants of sin, *but as sons of God.* As we continue in His word, we become more like Him and the shackles fall off, one by one. This is the brilliance of God's strategy, to make us free through the triumph of the Lamb.

4) Finally, Jesus came to proclaim the acceptable year of the Lord

This means that we have a chance for a new start. Why is the New Year such a big deal for so many people? Every New Year, people all over the world do two things:

1. Wish each other a happy and prosperous New Year;

2. Make resolutions to do things to improve their lives, such as quit smoking, lose weight, break off bad relationships, start a career etc.

It is almost as if people are fed up with their lives and the problems they caused for themselves, and are desperately trying to become better people, in the new year. A new year provides the hope of a new start. While a small percentage of people actually follow through and achieve some of what they resolve to do, the vast majority of New Year's resolutions never make it past January. We soon realize that New Year's resolutions are like fairy tales. As soon as the clock strikes twelve, the carriage becomes a pumpkin and we go back to being our old selves.

Jesus didn't come to preach a new year based on new resolutions, but an *acceptable* or delightful year, based on a new life. Here is a description of the experience that so many are desperately searching for, on midnight, December 31st, year after year:

> Therefore, if any one is in Christ, he is a new creation; old things have passed away; behold all things have become new. (2nd Corinthians: 5:17)

If only we could find a way to put our disappointing,

depressing past behind us and start over with a fresh, new life. That is exactly what God's strategic plan provides for us. Being in Christ, that is, accepting Him as God's plan for us and committing to live according to His word changes everything. Our IQ does not increase. We don't get any taller, better looking or richer. But the very change that the world desperately seeks in empty wishes, occurs on the inside.

As we apply God's word to our lives, we are changed on the inside and our old desires are replaced by a new desire to do what is pleasing to Him. There is no logic to this, it happens supernaturally, as God begins to transplant your old human nature with that of the Lamb. This is what real change is, old things are dead and we start a new life, without having to carry the burden of our sin. It can happen at any time we chose to reach out to God in faith. This is the good news that Jesus came to tell us, that the acceptable year of the Lord, *is now at hand!*

In this chapter, we were able to establish that God's strategic plan is relevant not just for today, but for all time, as it addresses the issue of sin and answers man's question about the meaning and value of life. We also saw that Jesus' sacrifice as the Lamb of God secured significant, life-changing benefits for us, including:

- An **eternal hope** for men of all races and circumstances, through the gospel or the good news;

- **Healing** for our broken hearts and lives;

- **Deliverance** and freedom from captivity and slavery to sin;

- **A new life**, a new beginning, the acceptable year of

the Lord.

As we learn to walk in this freedom, we begin to realize just how important and strategic we are, individually, to God. God's plan is not just to redeem and set us free, but to empower us to be His agents in the earth. Each of us has a place and a function that is of critical importance to God, not just in this life, but in the next.

We will examine this further, as we consider the role we play in executing God's plan in "Follow me and I will make you fishers of men."

CHAPTER 11

"FOLLOW ME AND I WILL MAKE YOU FISHERS OF MEN"

God's Strategic Plan contains tremendous benefits for us, as it not only provides us with salvation, deliverance, hope and peace, but through it, God has undertaken to provide for our physical needs as well (Philippians 4:19). This covers a range of human issues, including health, relationships and finances (an interesting topic for another day). The promise to meet our needs is not a blank check; *God does require us to do things His way and not ours.*

The plan of salvation shows us how to establish a personal relationship with God, based on trust and faith in Him. Unlike all other strategic plans, this is a living document; it not only tells us what to do, but its very words, provide the inspiration and motivation to do what God requires of us. Jesus said:

"The words that I speak to you, they are spirit and they are life"
(John 6:63)

Just as God's word created life on the earth in the beginning, it creates life in us now, as we believe and act on it. It is impossible to fully describe all that God has made available to us through faith in Him. The Apostle Paul explains it like this:

> But as it is written: Eye has not seen, nor ear heard, nor have entered into the heart of man the things which God has prepared for those who love Him.
> (1 Corinthians 2: 9)

Think of the vastness of the universe, the billions of stars and planets out there. Now imagine the limitless power that created *all that*, directed at puny us. Our limited minds are just not capable of absorbing all that God has prepared for those who embrace Him and His plan for our lives. As Jesus said, if we, being human parents, delight in giving our children good gifts, how much more would our Heavenly Father give good things to those that ask Him (Matthew 7:11).

We now come to the final part of God's Strategic Plan: *The Execution.* To explain what this is, we need to look at how strategic plans work in practice. A lot of thought and preparation go into constructing a strategic plan, even a simple one.

For example, assume you wanted to start a business; open a small restaurant. Your planning process would include setting objectives, working out a strategy, making an investment and then bringing it all to fruition in the execution of your plan. Here is what this might look like:

1) Objectives:
The first thing would be to define your objectives, which in this case may quite simply be to establish a family-owned restaurant in downtown Atlanta.

2) Strategy:
The next thing you do, is devise your strategy. This is where you figure out the details. Do you want to buy an existing restaurant, or start your own from scratch? Where would be the best place to locate this business? How big will the restaurant be? How many customers are you catering for? What is the menu? Who are your competitors? Based on your answers to questions like these, you would determine your best course of action or strategy.

3) Investment:
After you work out these details, you need to quantify the amount of investment required to ensure that you have enough capital to get the business off the ground and make it sustainable.

4) Execution:
The final stage is execution. This is where everything comes together, the plan is activated and where the work takes place. You find the physical location, negotiate the lease, do the renovations, hire the staff, buy the supplies, and promote the restaurant. After your restaurant is open, you now have the daily job of executing your plan, serving your customers and running your business every day.

God's strategic plan was constructed in very much the same way. His primary objectives were to destroy the works of darkness and free man from bondage to sin. His strategy was to create a people on earth, execute judgment on the devil and send His Son in the flesh, to set the captives free. The investment He made was through the sacrifice of the life of the Lamb.

Now we come to the final stage of His plan, *execution*. God wants to make this plan effective on the earth as a beneficial intervention to save *all* men. When

Jesus said "It is finished" and died on the cross, man's salvation became a completed work. The Apostle Paul confirms that there is nothing that we can, or need, to add to Jesus' sacrifice to make it any more complete.

> For there is only one God and one Mediator between God and men, the Man Christ Jesus, who gave Himself a ransom for all, to be testified in due time.
> (1Timothy 2:5-6)

Jesus is the only means of salvation for man and there is nothing more we can do to earn God's forgiveness. There is no other means of access to God, other than through Jesus. Not everyone understands this. Some believe that the better we are as a person, the more credit we generate towards earning God's grace.

We are conditioned to think like that from young. As children we were led to believe that if we were "good", a supernatural being, "Saint Nicholas" will visit us on Christmas Eve and give us presents, but if were we "bad", we would get nothing. This may all seem like innocent fun and a way of bringing joy and excitement to the lives of children, but at its core lies a spiritual deception.

Doing good deeds is commendable, *but it does not count as an antidote to sin.* If I were the most respected, most religious, honest person on earth and dedicated my life to serving others, I still would not be good enough to earn God's acceptance.

In the eyes of man, I may be a "saint", but in the eyes of God's justice, I would be nothing more than a well-behaved sinner. While society may recognize me as being more noble and praiseworthy than my fellow human beings, the sentence of death would still apply, because of my sin. The scripture does not say that the "wages of sin is death," but if I live a "good, clean life, God will take that into account". Often, at a funeral, a loved one would read a eulogy, outlining all the good the deceased did in his or her lifetime. While all of that may be true and comforting, I am sorry to say that this is not God's criterion for salvation.

I know that this may be hard for some to hear, but God does not operate a system of checks and balances. He does not weigh the good I've done against the bad, to see if I am worthy to enter His Kingdom. There is no "Saint Peter" standing at the "pearly gates" waiting to interview us for entry into heaven. We either stand in Christ alone, or stand on our own, to be judged and sentenced, according to the law of sin and death. This is exactly why God had to enact a strategic plan to save man.

While God's plan of salvation is complete and available to all men, there is one condition that must be satisfied by us. **We must sign up to take part in it.** Enrollment in God's plan is based on a limited time offer that expires on the day that we die. We must hear, believe and incorporate God's plan into our lives, on our own accord, *in the here and now.*

> "For God so loved the world, that He gave His only begotten Son that whoever believes in Him should not perish but have everlasting life."
> (John 3:16)

Notice the condition of "whoever believes". The truth is that, while Jesus did die on the cross for all men, no one in the world is automatically saved from sin. To receive God's forgiveness, we each have to believe in His Son, *personally and individually.*

Now, there are different levels of belief. Some people believe that Jesus was a good person with outstanding qualities. Others believe that Jesus is just one of the ways to God. If you asked people from both of these groups, "Do you *believe* in Jesus?" they would answer, "Yes, of course." That is not the kind of belief that God wants from us. He is looking for a belief that commits. Remember the covenant God made with Abraham? The question God asked Abraham was, in essence, "Do you believe in Me and trust Me enough, to put the life of your precious son in my hands?" God was not looking for a "yes" or "no" answer, but a demonstration of faith. Abraham had to commit to the act, in order to express his faith. Faith without action (or works) is no faith at all, but lip service and therefore dead (James 2:17).

God does not set a standard for us that He does not adhere to Himself. He demonstrated His love for us, in that, while we were still sinners, *Christ died for us.* God backed His strategic plan by making the ultimate commitment to it. That is what scripture means by "believe".

For us, belief in Jesus means that we acknowledge that we are sinners, that we repent of our sin and accept Jesus as our one and only Savior. Then comes the daily process of *yielding* the intentions and purposes of our hearts, completely to Him.

That is how God's Great Strategic Plan of Salvation is activated and developed in our lives. **We first have to believe and then to yield.**

The term *yield* has the same meaning as in traffic situations. When we see that sign at an intersection, we are required to come to a stop and allow the other car the right of way. Yielding to God means that we stop doing things our way and let God's Holy Spirit have the right of way in our decisions. To the world, believing is seeing, but to the redeemed, ***believing is yielding.***

Now that we understand how God's plan is applied to us and how important it is to the entire human race, we now have to figure out how to get the message out. This is the final stage of God's strategy, revealing what He has done for us all to the world. Unless God's plan is communicated to man, it is of no benefit to mankind.

> But even if our gospel is veiled, it is veiled to those who are perishing, whose minds the god of this world has blinded, who do not believe, lest the light of the gospel of the glory of Christ, who is the image of God, should shine on them.
> (2 Corinthians 4:3-4)

God sent His son to die for the world. But the only way the people of the world are going to know this, is if someone tells them. If this truth is kept secret, hidden or veiled, the solution that God has developed for man will be lost to people who are dying in sin. God has decided, in His wisdom, that the way this plan will be communicated to mankind, is through human contact. Although this plan is perfect in every respect, it does have one limitation: *us*.

This is why the Apostle Paul was so relentless in getting us to understand the importance of preaching the gospel.

> How shall they call on him in whom they have not believed? And how shall they believe in Him of whom they have not heard? And how shall they hear without a preacher?
> (Romans 10:14)

God's roll out strategy for His plan of salvation is to use those who believe, to reach out to others who have not yet heard the good news. It was Jesus Himself who initiated the process by instructing His disciples to:

"Go ye into all the world and preach the gospel to every creature."
(Mark 16:15).

This responsibility is passed down from one generation of believers to the next. Every generation of believers is responsible for preaching the gospel to the people in its own time. There have been times in the past when carrying out this responsibility could cost you dearly.

In a more barbaric time, men and women of the gospel have been beheaded, crucified and eaten by lions, for preaching the very things we are considering now. Even today in some cultures, publicly acknowledging Christ could land you in prison or expose you to state-sanctioned victimization.

Why would this seemingly harmless idea that Jesus died for the sin of the world cause such a violent response? Remember that although Satan has been defeated by the Lion of Judah he is still present in the affairs of men. He of all creatures, understands the importance of the gospel to man's salvation. His new strategy is to attack the gospel to either stop its spread altogether, blunt it by imposing other doctrines, or dilute its massage by suggesting scenarios other than Christ and Him crucified.

Satan knows he's condemned and he wants to take as many people as possible to judgment with him. That is his new game. His strategy is now modified away from attempting to defeat God, to doing two things:

1. Deceiving as many as possible into thinking that God's plan is not real.

2. Stopping God's marketing and distribution department, the Church, from doing its job.

1) Satan's strategy to deceive the world:

Satan uses a combination of force and persuasion to attack the gospel in our time. Even today he is able to lock the gospel out of some cultures by brute force. In other parts of the world the barbaric tactics he applied for many generations, are no longer tolerated by society. As a result, he has returned to his serpentine subtlety and is attempting to deceive people in the "free world" by the same logical persuasions he used on Eve. Here are some of his tools of deception to keep as many people as possible, away from the gospel.

Deception 1: "All roads lead to Rome":

At the height of the Roman Empire, all roads were in fact constructed to either lead directly, or via connectors, back to the center of world dominance, Rome. Since this was once a fact, Satan has twisted it to appear as an eternal truth.

The idea is that if God is the center of man's worship, how could anyone be so narrow minded to think that Christianity is the only way to Him? What about the billions of other people who believe in another road? Surely God loves all people and will accept us no matter what route we take to get to Him.

This "all roads to Rome" concept, which was true for a time, is not eternally true. Today, all roads do not lead to Rome just as all faiths do not lead to God. Jesus had a very, very, narrow, uncompromising perspective of the way to get to God. Here are some of His thoughts on the matter:

"I am the way the truth and the life. No one comes to the Father except through me"
(John 14:6)

"I am the light of the world. He who follows me shall not walk in darkness, but have the light of life" (John 8:12)

"Enter by the narrow gate; for wide is the gate and broad is the way that leads to destruction and there are many who go in by it; because narrow is the gate which leads to life and there are few who find it."
(Matthew 7:13-14)

Throughout His life on earth Jesus kept telling the Jews, "I am God, My Father and I are one, I am the light of the world, I am the bread of life, I am the only way to God, I am the only truth that there is". This made Him public enemy number one in His day and eventually led to His death. The message that Jesus is the only way is certainly not going to be popular in our world today.

The Apostle Peter told the Jews:

Nor is there salvation in any other, for there is no other name under heaven given among men by which we must be saved.
(Acts 4:12)

While God embraces diversity in that He loves all people, He is also a God of exclusivity since He has provided us with only one way to get to Him. We don't get to change the rules.

Deception 2: Man's achievement is the new golden calf.

In Exodus, chapter 32, Moses left the people to go to the mountain to receive the law from God. In his absence, the Jews melted the gold they brought out of Egypt, made a golden calf as a deity, and worshipped it.

141

Today, man worships all forms of golden calves. Satan has led many to believe that because God is not visible, He is not real and therefore they direct their worship to things that they can touch and taste and feel, such as personal achievements, education, success, and power.

We teach our children that in order to be successful in today's competitive world, they need to be educated. While this is very true, education has, for some, become the means by which we can achieve independence from everyone else, including, in some cases from God.

The more success we achieve the better off we are financially and the easier it is to focus our lives on success and financial rewards and forget about God. This is a subtle deception since it takes a truth and twists it into a lie. Our academic achievements do not make us independent from God, nor does it resolve the issue of personal consequence for sin. Another source of deception is the drive for position, promotion and power. Power and position are good, when used properly.

Compare and contrast the leadership styles of the patriarch Joseph with that of Herod of Judea. Joseph was second in authority only to pharaoh in Egypt. He was a man of immense power in the land. Yet he remained humble before God, recognizing that it was God's purpose that promoted him in the first place.

Herod, on the other hand, acquired and retained power by stealth and ruthless cunning. To him, power was a drug which placed him high above everyone else, including God. The problem with our world today is that there are more Herods in positions of power than Josephs. Once this happens, God's agenda in the earth is pressed down by the decisions of governments, presidents and kings.

2: Satan's attack on the Church.

While Satan is working on the minds of those who do not yet believe to keep them in darkness, he is also working on the Church to blunt its effectiveness as God's exclusive distributor of His strategic plan. To understand Satan's strategy against the Church, we need to understand how this group came into being and what its purpose is.

Before Jesus ascended into heaven, He called His disciples together and gave them instructions to go into all of the world and preach the gospel. But He also told them, before they set out, they should wait in Jerusalem (Acts 1:4-5) for the promise of the Father, the baptism of the Holy Ghost.

Acts Chapter 2 tells us that on the day of Pentecost, the disciples were together in a room praying and the Holy Ghost fell upon them and they spoke in other tongues. This first group of disciples followed Jesus' instructions and spread the gospel wherever they went. This led to other groups developing with the same mission and associating themselves together as the "Church" or "called out ones" (from the Greek "ekklesia"). Groups of Christians formed in different cities and locations and became known as the church in that location.

Jesus said he was going to establish this group even before He died. In Matthew 16:18, Jesus said that He was going to "build my church and the gates of hell shall not prevail against it." Some people believe that Jesus said that He was going to build His Church on Peter. I am not versed in Greek, but the difference in the words used in this statement, "Petros" (Peter) and "petra" the rock that Jesus referred to, suggests otherwise.

What is certain, is that from a strategic point of view, God will not build His Church using any man as a foundation, even one saved by grace. This is because the

Church is the key to the distribution of God's strategic plan and message. To build this on any foundation other than the infallible Christ, would be a strategic blunder of enormous proportions on God's part. Satan would destroy the Church and its message as easily as he destroyed Peter's faith in the courtyard after Jesus was arrested. God's plan is perfect in every regard and it is not built on the good intentions of imperfect men.

Jesus gave us a glimpse of the purpose of the church that He was building, when He said, *"and the gates of hell will not prevail against it."* It appears from this, that Jesus intends that the Church challenge and storm the gates of hell, the dominion of the devil.

God was about to empower a group of people with the Holy Spirit to enforce the victory that the Lion of Judah won on the earth. This returns man to the position of spiritual authority in the earth, as it was intended in the beginning. The Church is God's enforcement agency against the devil and the means by which the gospel will be distributed to all men.

To withstand the power of the devil, this entity must be built on a solid foundation, Christ Himself. No man, not even the righteous Job, and certainly not the impetuous Peter, is capable of kicking down the gates of hell on his own.

Building the Church using Peter as a foundation would be fine, if the purpose of the Church was purely to provide social programs or take care of the poor. But if the primary purpose of the Church is to withstand the gates of hell, then there is only one person who qualifies to be its foundation, and that is the Lion Himself. Jesus confirms this, *"I* will build *my* church."

The purpose of the Church is, therefore, to:

1) Storm the gates of hell (Mathew 16:18)

The commission that Jesus gave His disciples included preaching the gospel, casting out devils and laying hands on the sick. *These are the very same activities that He undertook as the Lion, when taking the fight to the devil.* It indicates that although the devil is legally condemned, he is still at large in the earth. The Church's job now is to reclaim the territory that Satan annexed as his own. Paul, in explaining this further, indicated that the Church's fight is not with flesh and blood (people) but with demonic forces, principalities powers and spiritual wickedness in high places (Ephesians 6:12).

2) Spread the news of God's Strategic plan via preaching the gospel (Mark 16:15)

The Church is the distribution network for the dissemination of God's strategic plan, the gospel. This is what the early Church in the book of Acts did and it should be our priority now. Preaching the gospel requires movement and action, "go" and "preach". Although this activity is still carried out by today's Church, I believe that there needs to be a renewed sense of urgency and commitment to moving outside our comfort zones and becoming more invasive.

It seems that the organizational structure of the modern Church is built around "come and hear", rather than "go and preach". The church is no longer a novel entity and people will not automatically come to us. We need to find ways to go to them, starting in our local community. We also need to teach believers to present their faith in a plausible, convincing manner. This is what Peter recommends to us on the matter:

> But sanctify the Lord God in your hearts, and always be ready to give a defense to every one who asks you a reason of the hope that is in you, with meekness and fear.
> (1 Peter 3:15)

We all have a corporate, as well as a personal obligation, to ensure that we set our priorities and programs in accordance with God's strategic plan and agenda.

3) Act as a nursery to help believers find their purpose in God

> And He Himself gave some to be apostles, some prophets, some evangelists and some pastors and teachers, for the equipping of the saints for the work of the ministry, for the edifying of the body of Christ.
> (Ephesians 4:11-12)

God has appointed various offices in the church to address the needs of His people. Jesus said that He is the vine and we are the branches (John 15:5). The vine nourishes the branches and the branches produce the fruit. Healthy branches produce healthy fruit. It is the duty of the leadership of the Body to ensure that the flock is provided with sound doctrine, wise counsel and Godly example.

Satan knows that his new enemy in the earth is the Church and his plan is to stop this group from carrying out its mission for God. Here are some of the counter measures that Satan uses against the church:

Complacency:

Then Jesus said unto them, "Take heed and beware of the

leaven of the Pharisees and Sadducees.
(Matthew 16:6)

Jesus warned the disciples to beware the leaven of the Jewish clergy. Paul repeats that same warning to the church in I Corinthians 5:6. Many scholars consider that "leaven", or yeast, applies to false doctrine and Jesus was warning the disciples and the church to be wary of false teaching contaminating the body. While this may very well be true, I believe that it goes further than this.

I believe that Jesus was also warning us to be careful of adopting a complacent attitude that could infect the body, making it bloated, lazy and ineffective. The Pharisees were supposed to be knowledgeable authorities on God's law and ways in the day of Jesus. While they had a strong claim to intellectual knowledge of the law, they completely missed the spirit in their practice of religion. As a result, they became self-righteous, spiritually arrogant and held themselves to be morally and spiritually superior to other men.

Jesus warns us today about developing that attitude. The devil is only too willing to dangle position, prestige and power before church leaders, to get them to lose sight of God's focus and develop one of their own. Remember this is exactly what he attempted with Jesus in the wilderness.

Satan uses complacency to get a church that is engaged in leading people out of darkness, to slip into neutral and stop moving forward. There is nothing wrong with building funds, family fun nights and social programs. However, these things must not distract the leadership of the body from spending time and effort, thinking, praying and working on reaching out to their communities *and going there* to meet the needs of the lost.

Time wasting:

Jesus' proposition to the early disciples was, "Follow me and I will make you fishers of men". This is still the recruitment poster for believers today. Now that we understand that God is working with a plan to save man, we need to realize that He is also on a timetable and there is a sense of urgency in each generation to get the job done. According to 2 Corinthians 6:2, now is the acceptable time, today is the day of salvation.

In the parable of the talents (Matthew 25:14-30), Jesus tells of a businessman who entrusts different levels of resources, called talents, to each of three different employees or servants. At the end of the parable, the master is particularly harsh on the servant who takes the resource and does nothing with it. Although that servant was not as gifted as the other two, he did not even make an effort to use the money that the master entrusted to him.

Now we often think of the talent in terms of money or wealth. But its most potent application is in time. Time is a scarce resource that God gives to each of us. Exactly how much time we have, no one but God knows. What he is looking for, however, is for us to use what we have, to achieve His purpose as best as we can. I know that we are all guilty of wasting time in the past, but it is not too late to change our attitude and priorities. One approach is to start every day with this prayer attitude: "Lord, this is a new day, a new opportunity to walk in Your purpose. Help me to be sensitive to Your presence and leading as I go about my daily routine. Help me to make this day count for eternity."

Division:

One of the most potent weapons of the enemy, is to sow seeds of division among different groups of believers, collectively called the Church. I have noticed that church membership is often divided on the basis of color and race. I fully understand that the Church is no longer a purely spiritual entity and that even in Paul's day there were issues of ethnic identities influencing the gathering of the saints. I also agree that people are likely to associate with groups with which they feel common bonds. But at the end of the day, we are all part of the same body. The Apostle Paul emphasized this point to the Ephesians:

> There is one body and one Spirit, just as you were called in one hope of your calling; One Lord, one faith, one baptism; one God and Father of all, who is above all and through all and in you all.
> (Ephesians 4:4-6)

If we all share the same faith, the same hope, the same calling, under one God, why are we so divided? I believe that the devil has come up with a clever trick to create and stir up division in the body and weaken the effectiveness of the Church.

It is apparent that, here in the US, we take our politics very seriously indeed, as well as we should. Politics affects policies, which in turn affect us all. It is no secret too that political affiliations, ethnicity and social class, are sometimes associated together. This has led to a very noticeable distinction between some Churches in the same communities.

My question is: What do our political differences have to do with God's strategic plan? When a person joins the military, all of the distinctions about race, class and political affiliations are "checked at the door". It doesn't matter who you are, what your color is, or whether you are a Democrat or a Republican, the person fighting by your side is your brother-in-arms. You live together, fight together and sometimes die together, for one cause, facing one common enemy.

Facing a common enemy eliminates all the artificial distinctions we bring to the table. The Church has a common enemy, but he has cleverly brought in other distinctions to distract us and get us to magnify human differences that cause us to be at variance with each other. Once this happens, we erect man-made walls called denominations, and then we pretend that those with names different from ours do not exist.

I believe that Satan elects not to persecute the modern Church with one common cause of action (at least not yet), because he knows that this will unite the factions and denominations, as one Body, against him. He has adopted a sort of "let sleeping dogs lie" approach to blunting the effectiveness of the Church. God hasten the day when the barriers in the Body, which keep us separated, are destroyed.

Please don't think that I am being critical of Church leaders. The men and women who take on the responsibility to lead, teach, mentor and disciple God's people, stand in the shoes of the first apostles and the early Church elders. Even back then there were differences of opinion among leaders as to how the Body should function and it is clear that none of the early apostles were above correction and re-direction. The Apostle Paul tells us:

> Now when Peter had come to Antioch, I withstood him to his face, because he was to be blamed, for before certain men came from James, he would eat with the Gentiles, but when they came, he withdrew and separated himself, fearing those who were of the circumcision. And the rest of the Jews also played the hypocrite with him, so that even Barnabas was carried away with their hypocrisy.
> (Galatians 2:11-12)

What a highly charged situation. The Apostle Peter being called out and chastised "to his face" by Paul in front of the entire congregation ("I said to Peter before them all"- verse 14). Peter had made a grievous error which threatened the purity of fellowship and the unity of the saints. He had, in a moment of weakness, allowed his Jewish heritage to create division among the believers by refusing to eat with Gentile Christians in order to appease certain Jews.

The two things we note from this passage of Scripture, are that Paul was mature enough to correct him and Peter was humble enough to recognize his error and submit to proper direction. These I believe, are important considerations for all those who take on the responsibility of leading the flock.

It is human weakness that causes us to place heritage, political views, race, social status and other earthly considerations above the pure requirements of God's purpose. What is clear from Paul's uncompromising tone as he addresses Peter and the Galatian church, is that God takes His strategic plan very seriously and He is not playing when it comes to addressing issues of stewardship. So, *beware of the leaven of the Pharisees.*

In this chapter, we looked at how God's strategic plan impacts man and the responsibility of the Church to be the vehicle through which God's grace and the good news of the gospel are shared in this generation. God's plan to save man is truly incredible. It was worked out with care and precision, over the course of thousands of years, just for our benefit. What is even more amazing is that God not only has a plan to save mankind, but has also crafted a specific purpose for each of us, *individually.*

Our next chapter, entitled, "What's my destiny Mama?" will look at God's strategic plan as it applies to us personally and how we can know our purpose in life.

CHAPTER 12

"WHAT'S MY DESTINY MAMA?"

In the 1994 movie, *Forrest Gump*, the main character, Forrest, played by Tom Hanks, asks his mother a question for the ages, "What's my destiny, Mama?" While this quote does not make the top ten list of most famous Gump quotes, it is to me, the most meaningful. This is a question that most of us ask at some point in our lives. What is my destiny? Where is my life (career, business, ministry, relationship, marriage, family) heading?

My first recollection of ever considering the question of the meaning of life and the future that lay before me, goes back to my childhood years, when I first heard the lyrics of the classic song *"Que Sera Sera"*, performed by the enchanting Doris Day. I can very vaguely remember my own mother, Marilyn, singing it to me as a child. "The future's not ours to see, Que sera, sera."

The question of destiny came up again later in my life, this time, as a more serious and urgent issue. When I was 18 and was just finishing high school, I was unsure of what my next steps should be. I became very concerned that, unlike many of my friends, I had not yet made a decision on a possible career direction. I eventually asked my father, Victor, who was also an accountant, what he thought I should do. His response was, "Whatever you do, as long as it is honest work and you do your best at it, you would do well." Although my father did not answer my question specifically, he did provide me with clear direction.

Why are we so concerned about what the future holds for us?

I believe that deep down, people everywhere, regardless of nationality, race, or creed, want the same things out of life. We all want to live in peace instead of war, to be free rather than be in bondage, to be happy instead of sad, to be healthy instead of sick, to have purpose and fulfillment in life, rather than frustration and disappointment. The problem is that life is uncertain. Uncertainty makes us uncomfortable because it creates the risk that things might not turn out, as we would like. As a result, we seek assurances from those around us that our lives will turn out well and that everything would be just fine.

But what does "just fine" mean and how do we assess whether things are going well for us? We live in a material world and for many of us, destiny is related to material things. For those who are poor, destiny becomes a search for a way out of poverty and the hope of a better life. The main reason that people migrate from less developed countries to more developed ones, is to search for a destiny that is measured by a better standard of living. This is not a new phenomenon; it has been taking place in countries like the US, Canada and all over Europe for centuries.

It is natural for all of us to want to improve the quality of our lives and give our children a better future than we have. But to do this, we very often have to face adversity and overcome challenges along the way. Here are some people who stand out as having succeeded despite the odds:

- Andrew Carnegie, the steel magnate, born 1835 to a poor family in Scotland, who later became the richest man in the world;

- Henry Ford born 1863, who started and failed in five business ventures, and went bankrupt five times, before starting the Ford Motor Company;

- Ursula Burns, Chairman and CEO of Xerox, born 1958 to a poor New York family, went on to become the first African American woman to lead a Fortune 500 company.

People like these provide the inspiration to others, to aspire to destinies beyond their existing circumstances. So the issue of "What's my destiny?" or "Where is my life heading?" will be an ageless question asked by each passing generation. But how do we actually go about finding our destiny? Are there any proven methods or approaches that we can consider?

Here are two that come to mind:

Option 1:
"When life gives you lemons, you make lemonade". Life is *uncertain*, or, according to Forrest Gump, "like a box of chocolates." You don't know what the future holds, but to

succeed in life, you take what you get and create your own destiny.

Option 2:
There is a path for your life, a *certain* destiny, laid out by God before you. You can search it out and walk in it.

Let us evaluate both of these to see which works better for us:

Life is uncertain and when it gives you lemons, you make lemonade.

This is a common-sense approach to finding destiny and is adopted by many people. It is based on the premise that life is a combination of good and bad experiences. "Good things" (e.g. being born into wealth or with a brilliant mind) produce good destinies. "Bad things", (e.g. being born to poor parents, or a lack of education opportunities) if left unaddressed, will tend to stifle your true potential and derail your destiny. As a result, if life serves up something unpleasant (a lemon), find a way to overcome it and use it to your advantage.

Here are some famous quotes that typify how the world sees and explains what destiny is:

- "The only person you are destined to become is the person you decide to be." Ralph Waldo Emerson.

- "Destiny is not a matter of chance, it is a matter of choice. It is not a thing to be waited for, it is a thing to be achieved." William Jennings Bryan.

- "I am the master of my own fate, / I am the captain of my own soul." William Ernest Henley.

Based on the above, it appears that if we want to achieve our destiny, we must be pro-active. We must take control of our circumstances and shape our own future to achieve what we want out of life. This is, in fact, the advice that many people receive from their mentors. Most of what we have been told, or read for ourselves, on the subject of destiny would probably sound like this:

- You can be whatever you want to be.

- Nothing is impossible if you believe in yourself and work hard to achieve your dreams.

- "What the mind can conceive and believe, it can achieve." - Napoleon Hill

It is true that hard work and determination, together with finding the right opportunities, can make us successful in this world, and there are many people who have created their own destiny this way. There are many motivational books, speakers and life coaches who offer suggestions and guidance on how to do this. Most of these involve us identifying what we want to achieve in life (setting personal objectives and goals), assessing where we are now, our individual strengths and weaknesses and then devising a plan of action to move from where we are now, to where we want to be.

Much of this is based on sound personal planning practice and usually works in helping us focus on what we consider important in our lives and commit to changing unproductive habits and attitudes. For example, your teenaged child comes to you after watching an exciting episode of *Law and Order* (or for those who can remember that far back, *Perry Mason*) and says, "I want to be a lawyer." Your response would probably be, "Sure honey, but if you really want to be a lawyer, you need to start focusing on your grades in school *now.*"

This is good practical advice, and it is how many people eventually find their direction in life. We first figure out what we want, and then set about getting it. The problem is that this works only up to a point and suffers from two main limitations:

1. We may think we know what we want, but is *that* the best thing for us?

2. What happens when we can't create our destiny to fit what we want?

Do we really know the difference between what we want and what is best for us?

The world has its own warning label for the things we pursue in life, *"be careful what you wish for, you just might get it"*. Very often, the things that we are attracted to, or find desirable, come with adverse emotional and spiritual side effects. Having a career is great, *but your career is not your destiny* and if you make it your exclusive focus as some do, it can extract a painful price on your personal life. Being wealthy is great, but if you make the pursuit of wealth your destiny or destination, you may find that you don't like the person you have become.

What happens when things don't work out the way we want?

In addition to not always knowing what is best for us, we are not always able to achieve what we desire for ourselves, no matter how hard we try. Many children labor under the expectations of their parents, who see a destiny for them, which they are just not capable of achieving. This sometimes becomes an issue in families with a professional or academic tradition. A child is born into a family of professionals, where the parents and the siblings are all doctors. This particular child, however, does not have the academic ability to succeed in the medical field. If the parents are not careful, he/she can go through life thinking and feeling that they are a failure and a disappointment to the family. Huge self-esteem issues flow out of pushing ourselves and our children to become things that we/they are not destined to be.

I believe, therefore, that the fatal flaw in the "create your own destiny" approach is that success in life is not measured so much by what you achieve, but by who you are *and the type of person you have become*. The world evaluates success in material terms and drives us towards our goals by encouraging us to always want more. We are encouraged to want a better car, a bigger house, earn more money, be more popular, acquire more wealth, exercise more influence, improve the way we look. It appears difficult for many of us to say, "This is enough!" and as a result, we spend our entire lives in pursuit of *a destiny of more*.

There is nothing wrong with wanting better things for ourselves and our children. Be aware, though, that having better things does not make you a better person. If this were so, every wealthy, successful person would live a happy, contented life. There are many people who have dedicated their lives to becoming a "something" or a "somebody", and having achieved their objective, realize that success does not fill the vacuum in their souls.

American poet, writer and philosopher, Henry D. Thoreau, explained it like this, **"The mass of men lead lives of quiet desperation."**

What a mental image, *"quiet desperation."* This means that, on the outside we may appear calm, cool and in control of our lives, but on the inside, we are full of turmoil, doubt and self-loathing. This, I believe, is a consequence of the way that the world encourages us to pursue our destinies.

As Jesus said:

> "For what will it profit a man if he gains the whole world, and loses his own soul? Or what will a man give in exchange for his soul?"
> (Mark 8: 36-37)

It is my experience that "losing your soul" is not just an eternal consideration. Many of us are quietly losing little bits of our soul every day, as we continue to struggle to shape our destinies by ourselves and in our own way. It would seem that the world's approach to finding and fulfilling destiny does not always bring us the fulfillment we want in life. But is there a better plan, and if so, how do we find it?

I believe that there is a better, more certain way to finding our destiny in life, but to do this we have to go in the opposite direction that the world suggests and "let go and let God". This is probably the simplest, yet most difficult thing for us to do, since it requires us to not trust in ourselves and our own abilities, but rather to put our trust in God.

Finding your destiny is not about believing in yourself and trusting your instincts, but believing in God and trusting His purpose.

Your destiny is tied to God's purpose for you. Find God's

purpose for your life and you will find your destiny. Here is the assurance that God provides to get us to this point:

> Trust in the Lord with all your heart, and lean not unto your own understanding; In all your ways acknowledge Him and He shall direct your paths.
> (Proverbs 3:5-6)

There are many scripture verses that we should commit to memory and this one is at the top of the list. God has absolutely guaranteed that He will direct your path in life, according to His purpose for you, if you trust Him with all your heart and rely on Him, and not your-self, to shape your future.

God backs up this guarantee with another assurance:

> For I know the thoughts that I think towards you, says the Lord, thoughts of peace and not evil, to give you a future and a hope.
> (Jeremiah 29:11)

Putting these two together, here is what God is saying to each of us:

"I think about you *all the time* and I have a definite plan and destiny for you. This destiny is one that will bring you peace and will achieve specific goals in your life. To find this path, you have to do three things:

- Trust Me with all your heart;

- Don't place your confidence in your own wisdom, understanding and judgment, *but in me;*

- Consult me in every decision and situation; look to

me *and expect my guidance.*

If you do this, I guarantee that I will guide your life and give you purpose". This is the ultimate goal of God's strategic plan, to redeem man and give each of us a new life of purpose and hope. Does that mean that everything will go according to our plan and we live a life without challenges and problems? Not at all.

Jesus said that once we decide to follow after Him, we will face opposition and obstacles, sometimes more so than other people. In John 16:33, Jesus told His disciples that they will face tribulation and trials in the world, but they should be of good cheer, because He has overcome the world.

Our lives will always be a combination of good experiences and those that may be difficult, or challenge us in different ways. God knows this, but He does not want us to take matters into our own hands. He wants us to stop "bending ourselves out of shape" and trying to squeeze our lemons to make lemonade. His appeal, is for us to submit our challenges to Him, so He can work out a solution for us and lead us "in the path of righteousness for His name's sake."

This is what David was conveying to us in the 23rd Psalm. "The Lord is my shepherd, I shall not suffer want. He provides me with green pastures and leads me beside still waters. He restores my soul and secures my future. *My destiny is in His hands*". David knew this from personal experience. He was plucked from obscurity as a young shepherd boy, the last and least significant of Jesse's sons and anointed to be king of Israel. His sheer confidence in God, led him into one of the most famous face to face combat scenarios in history, the battle with Goliath.

David became a great king and it is from his line, that God sent His King to the earth. An amazing rags to riches story, more so than any of the other famous people we considered earlier. Although David was far from perfect, he always maintained an honest relationship with God and was willing to submit to God's correction in his life, no matter the consequences. Because of his willingness to submit, God personally guided David through every battle and trial in life and paid him the ultimate commendation. In Acts 13:22, the Apostle Paul confirms that God called David "a man after my own heart". What a testimony of destiny. This is exactly what God wants to create in each of us.

This is what destiny is all about, fulfilling God's strategic plan for our lives. It requires us to adopt His value system and not the world's. The world places value on destinies based on achievement, success and recognition. **God's value system is based on building Godly character in us.**

Dr. Ern Baxter (1914-1993), once said that *"God is more intent on the production of character than on the provision of comforts."* So true Dr. Baxter, so true.

God is ultimately after something specific in our lives and His plan of destiny draws this out of us over a lifetime of learning to submit to Him. The thing that He wants most for us is for Christ to be fully formed in us. That, to Him, is more important than any material blessing we can receive.

Yes, God will bless us and give us good things, because it is in His nature to provide for His people. But He doesn't want material things to choke us spiritually. He is more intent on the production of Godly character in us, because if we have this, then we can overcome any obstacle that stands in our way. Jesus said, "Be of good cheer, I have overcome the world." As we conform more to His image and likeness, so will we.

Now that we understand what destiny is, and the difference between a life molded by the world and one molded by God, we now come to the conclusion of our examination of God's strategic plan, where we consider what we must do as individuals to position ourselves to find our destiny in God.

CHAPTER 13

FINDING YOUR DESTINY IN GOD

We now come to the final chapter of this book. Everything we have considered so far, the whole Strategic Plan of God, leads to this single point: *finding our individual destiny.*

God's strategic plan is ultimately focused on us as individuals and in order to understand how to function as people of destiny, we need to review the guidance that scripture provides on the subject. Here are some building blocks that we must put in place to strengthen our walk with God and find our purpose in life.

Humility:
The walk of destiny is a walk of humility.

> He has shown you O man, what is good and what the Lord requires of you, but to do justly, and to love mercy and to walk humbly with your God."
> (Micah 6:8)

We must keep in mind, that when we walk with God, our accomplishments in life are not the product of our own abilities, intellect or talents, but rather, are the results of "God working in you to will and to do of His good pleasure" (Philippians 2:13). Any success we achieve is the result of God working in us, through us and for us. There are many people even Christians, who start out on life's course riding a wave of success, only to be defeated by the self-indulgence that sometimes accompanies fame and fortune.

God places a high premium on humility, so regardless of our station in life, we must ensure that we do not become arrogant or "puffed up" by the favor God extends to us along the way. Remember that "God resists the proud, but gives grace to the humble" (James 4:6).

Submission:
The walk of destiny is a walk of submission. The starting, middle and ending point of finding our destiny is coming to a place of submission to God. The more committed we are to living in submission the more potent God's working in our lives will be. Having the attitude, "Lord, have Your way in me; anything you require of me, I will do", gets better results than, "Lord, I hear what you're saying to me, but".

That reminds me of the rich young ruler in Mark 10:22, who one day came to Jesus, very excited about following Him. All of Jesus' disciples had forsaken their normal lives to live daily in His physical presence. Jesus told this young man the same thing He told Peter and the others, "Leave your everyday life behind and come follow me." The rich young ruler was "sad at that saying and went away grieved for he had great possessions." What a disaster. This young man, whose name will forever be irrelevant, gave up the opportunity to walk with

Jesus and have a life of divine destiny, because he was not willing to let go of his worldly destiny. God is merciful and He will be patient with us, but we have to be willing to submit to Him and purpose in our hearts to do so. The more we hold back of ourselves, the longer God's processes take and the less effective they are in our lives.

Consider the parable of the prodigal son in Luke 15:11-32. This young man was a son, just as we are. His father, a businessman, expected that all his sons would work in his business and help to expand his influence. Our Father also has a business and it is His strategic plan that we all work in His business to expand His Kingdom. This is a part of what makes up our destiny.

This young man was as stubborn as we are sometimes. He decided to leave his father's business and go off on a frolic of his own, wasting a lot of time and resources in unproductive pursuits. Scripture says that "when he came to himself" or when he came to his senses, he repented of his stubbornness and rebellion, and returned to his father's plan for his life. What God is saying to us is that it is never too late to come to our senses and commit to His strategic plan for our lives.

Forgetting:
The walk of destiny is a forward march. The key to moving forward is forgetting the past. There are some people who are tormented by their past. As soon as they make one step toward a destiny in God the devil reminds them of who they were, where they came from and what they did.

God does not reject us or limit our destiny because of our past. The problem is that we carry memories of previous failures and sin around with us, imbedded in our minds, which the devil dredges up to discourage us and slow us down. When this happens, recognize it as the devil speaking to you and not God. The world judges us based on our past; anyone with a record is to be treated with caution. God doesn't hold our past miss-deeds against us; He forgives them, so we can start over afresh. Consider the Apostle Paul.

Paul was the least likely candidate to be the oracle of God. If it were up to me, I certainly would not pick him. This man relentlessly persecuted and harassed the early church. In fact when he first converted to Christianity, the disciples were suspicious of him because they knew him to be someone who persecuted the believers. In Acts 22:20, Paul confesses to having consented to the stoning to death of God's servant Stephen, in fact he even held the clothes of those who carried out the act. Could you imagine the baggage that Paul brought into Christianity with him?

Here is his recommendation to people like us, with baggage:

> Brethern, I do count myself to have apprehended; but this one thing I do, forgetting those things which are behind, and reaching forth unto those things which are ahead, I press forward toward the goal for the prize of the upward call of
> God in Christ Jesus
> (Philippians 3:13-14)

This is the remedy for things from our past that seek to confound us in the present. Yield it to God, repent of the sin, make it right where possible and move on. The best way to forget your past is to make it right with God and then press on. However, a word of caution is needed. There are some things that occur between people that are so delicate it would take wise counsel to guide us through the process of making them right. Some past circumstances may be impossible to remedy.

In these situations, the best course is to seek Godly counsel if you feel convicted of any issue that you think is beyond your ability to address. While this may not be a comfortable thing to do, it is necessary that we admit past failures to God, seek counsel where needed and press forward to find His higher calling for us.

Start where you are:
The walk of destiny requires a first step and the best place to start is right where you are. Here is what Paul advises:

> Art thou called while a slave? Do not be concerned about it: but if you can be made free, rather use it.
> Art thou bound to a wife? Do not seek to be loosed. Are you loosed from a wife? Do not seek a wife.
> (1 Corinthians 7:21, 27)

The Apostle Paul recognized that we all find ourselves in different places in our lives when we begin our walk of destiny. God is no respecter of persons and His grace is extended to people of all walks of life with a whole range of different personal circumstances. God's call of destiny works from the inside out, not the other way around. As the Holy Spirit begins the work of transforming our hearts from within, the divine destiny that God has in store for us begins to manifest itself in our lives outwardly. As a result, there is no need to make radical changes to your life's circumstances *unless and until God specifically requires this of you.*

So, if you are pursuing a career, there is no need to stop. Prayerfully continue on your path and look for God's guidance along the way. You don't have to drop out of school, abandon your career, or to take extreme measures to find your divine destiny. As a matter of fact, God may want you exactly where you are, to use you to reach people who otherwise would not see the gospel in action. Our prayer must be "Lord, I offer you my life. Take it, change it and use it for your purpose and glory. Show me what I must do to walk in your will and to fulfill the destiny to which you have called me."

Offer God what you have:
The walk of destiny requires that we give our best. We all have different gifts, skills, talents and abilities. I have two teenaged daughters, one of whom, like her mother is gifted with a pitch perfect, voice. The other daughter takes after her daddy and can't carry a tune. The thing is that they both love to sing and I love to hear them sing. That's the way it is with God. He doesn't care about what we offer Him as long as we give Him our best.

Consider the little boy with the five loaves and two fish. In John 6:6-12, as Jesus was ministering to a large crowd, He realized that the people were with him for so long that they *had* to be hungry. He asked His disciples if there was any food to feed the crowd; their response was, "There is a lad here, who has five barley loaves and two small fish, but what are they among so many?" (John 6:9).

Jesus took the loaves and fish that the boy gave Him, offered it to God and the result was that thousands of people were fed and blessed. The lesson for us here is that every little thing you are and have is of strategic value to God, *if you willingly offer it to Him.*

You may think "I am not educated" or "I am just a simple person with no special talents or training". That may be true in the natural but remember that the people Jesus selected and trusted to carry out the great commission were not the educated priests, but simple ordinary fishermen. The one thing that the world will never be able to duplicate is the wisdom of God. When God's wisdom abides in you no amount of education can prevail against you. God delights in taking the simple things of the world to confound the wise. Your education, skills and talents, or lack thereof, are not a deterrent to God when you make yourself available to Him.

God will reveal your specific purpose in due time.
The walk of destiny reveals your purpose in life and helps you to fit in to the exact place God wants you to be.

> For you died and your life is hidden with Christ in God. (Colossians 3:3)

Water baptism symbolizes that we identify with the death and resurrection of Jesus. We are dead to the old life and risen to a new life in Christ. Your life and destiny are now hidden with Christ in God. It is there, it is real, *but it is hidden*. God will, over a process of time, reveal your destiny not just to you, but also to those who know you. Think of your walk in destiny as a rose that has not yet bloomed. All of the potential and beauty is hidden in the bud. As God brings the bud to maturity and perfection over time, it opens up to reveal the true beauty of the rose, which is His glory in our lives. This is how our destinies are revealed over time. Looking back, we will realize that those events and experiences in our lives which seemed unrelated and isolated, were in fact leading us in a particular direction towards a definite purpose.

The walk of destiny is a walk of faith.

> For we walk by faith not by sight.
> (2 Corinthians 5:7)

God almost never lays out our path or destiny for us in plain sight. If we had certain knowledge of how our lives will turn out, then we wouldn't have to trust God for anything. God places a high premium in our faith and trust in Him. Hebrews tells us,

> But without faith it is impossible to please Him, for he who comes to God must believe that He is, and is a rewarder of those who diligently seek Him.
> (Hebrews 11:6)

We have to walk by faith to find our destiny in God. Without faith we cannot please God and *we will not find the path He has laid out for us*. Now this is where the rubber meets the road; it is easy to trust God when we have a sense of the direction He is taking us and things are going well. My own personal experience is that when things are uncertain, when trouble arises in life, when we are unsure of what to do next, panic often sets in. So, here is some "do as I say but not as I (sometimes) do" advice. Anytime life becomes uncertain and the way becomes cloudy, realize immediately that you are already *in the middle* of a battle, a test, a trial. Here's what the Apostle James says about this:

> My brethren, count it all joy when you fall into various trials, knowing that the testing of your faith produces patience.
> (James1:2-3)

God often uses trials as a means of building endurance and patience in us so that we can rise up and fulfill our destinies. So when these come your way, view them as a spiritual workout, a means of exercising faith and drawing closer to God.

Lean on the examples of Abraham and Job and learn to walk by faith, not by sight, no matter how dark the road ahead may seem. Always keep your lines of communication with God open, especially in times of uncertainty and look for that sense of peace that He will give you, as an assurance that you are in His way and will. If at any time on the road to your destiny you feel overwhelmed by the challenges of life, remember what David said:

> Hear my cry O God; attend to my prayer. From the ends of the earth I will cry unto You, when my heart is overwhelmed; lead me to the rock that is higher than I. For You have been a shelter for me, a strong tower from the enemy. I will abide in Your Tabernacle forever; I will trust in the shelter of Your wings.
> (Psalm 61:1-4)

Trust in the shelter of His wings.

Don't become unequally yoked.
The walk of destiny requires us to be selective.

> Do not be unequally yoked together with unbelievers. For what fellowship has righteousness with lawlessness and what communion has light with darkness?
> (2 Corinthians 6:14)

This is a very important consideration as you forge ahead towards your destiny. Paul advises us not to become "unequally yoked together with unbelievers". The image he conveys is that of two or more oxen harnessed to pull together in the same direction. If the oxen are of different sizes or strengths, e.g. one is young and strong and the other is older and weak, the bond they form will be ineffective since they are not bringing the same values to the team.

The same applies with us. Our values as believers are different to non-believers. We want to live our lives to please the Lord and to find His purpose for us. Unbelievers cannot relate to this since their values come from the world and they march to the beat of a different drum.

Here are some examples of unequal yoking.

You are a single Christian endeavoring to serve the Lord. Along comes this attractive and charming person who smiles in your direction. You quickly realize that he/she does not share your faith or your values. He/she wants to establish a relationship that goes beyond being just casual friends. What do you do?

You want to start a business and the person that you are considering as a partner does not share your faith or your values. However he/she is a perfect business fit. What do you do?

In both these cases, the logical choice would be to proceed in the natural to explore the relationship. But scripture advises against even considering this, because spiritual conflicts *will* arise, and if you are already yoked it would be too late to change course, without causing yourself great hurt and damage. So, Christian singles, don't be be taken in by the flattery or the advances of an unequally yoked suitor. This applies even to someone who is part of the fellowship of believers. If you are considering a relationship, look beyond the external -*the physical, financial and natural*- and ask the Lord to give you spiritual discernment so you can assess the heart of your intended, and evaluate him or her for Godly character.

Likewise as a Christian business-owner who might be considering partnering with someone in business, you should be sure that you share a common bond in the faith and that your potential partner's ethics and vision for the business are in sync with yours and God's. Your business has a divine purpose and your partner must share this vision, or else there is likely to be discord.

Seek Him first

The walk of destiny requires us to put God first. Jesus said,

> "But seek first the kingdom of God and His righteousness and all these things shall be added unto you."
> (Matthew 6:33)

We don't have to revert to the spiritually dead strategy of creating our own destiny. What we should do is to put God first, advance His kingdom, stand up for what is right by God's definition and He will direct your path. God will add to us and mix in to our lives all of the ingredients we need to live with purpose. This is His promise and commitment to us. As we seek Him first and trust Him for the outcome to every venture, He will not only provide for us, but will guide us according to His will. Make the things of God a priority in your life and your destiny will be certain.

Stay connected to the vine

The walk of destiny will develop as we stay connected to the vine. Jesus said:

> "I am the vine, you are the branches: He that abides in Me and I in him, bears much fruit; for without Me you can do nothing." (John 15:5)

We have to stay connected to the vine in order to live above the frustrations of life. How do we do this? By developing a regular diet of feeding on God's word. God's word is spirit and life, food and drink to us. Jesus said that, "I am the bread of life, I am the living water that refreshes your soul."

I know from personal experience how frustrating life can be, when things fall apart around you. It seems at those times that God and His destiny for you are very far away. At times like these it is easy to fall into despair, but don't lose heart, God is still at work in you. He will never leave you or forsake you, just continue to trust Him. If you are at a place of "quiet desperation" in your spiritual life, make time to read and study God's word, and ask Him to refresh your soul and purpose.

Remember:

> Even the youths shall faint and be weary, and the young men shall utterly fall But those that wait upon the Lord shall renew their strength, they shall mount up on wings as eagles, they shall run and not be weary they shall walk and not faint. (Isaiah 40: 30-31)

Stay connected to the vine and you won't grow faint!

Develop the talent that is in you

The walk of destiny develops our talents. Paul encouraged Timothy to "stir up the talent" that was in him. This has a direct reference to spiritual gifts that God had given Timothy to enable him to function as a minister in the body of Christ.

God has given each of us spiritual gifts that are important to us being able to fulfill our destiny. These gifts are ministry gifts, designed to help others find their own destiny. In Ephesians 4:11, Paul identifies a number of functions which require gifting from God, such as pastors, apostles, prophets, teachers and evangelists.

You may think that none of these apply to you and maybe they don't, at least not yet. There is, however, one ministry function that applies to all of us regardless of personal abilities, and it is the ministry of "helps" (1 Corinthians 12:28).

I encourage *every Christian* to get involved in the ministry of helps. This ministry is, or in my opinion *should be,* the starting position for every servant of God and is the training ground for a destiny in God. You don't need to meet any special qualification to be in the ministry of helps other than a willingness to serve. The ministry of helps is anything that you can do to support the Strategic Plan of God.

In Acts 6:3, the early church was growing quickly and there was an urgent need to do the practical work of taking care of the widows in the church and waiting on tables. The apostles chose seven men whose only qualification for the job was that they were willing to do anything to serve God, and appointed them to the elevated status of waiters. Our human nature wants us to do things we think are important and esteemed by others. Every function in the Kingdom is important and recognized by God, even waiting tables, parking cars, greeting the saints, visiting the sick, and making time to lend support to a brother or sister in need.

What God values most in our work is our attitude. If we do these things willingly as unto Him they count for eternity. The ministry of helps is an important part of your destiny as it helps you to get connected to people at the simplest level, it builds character and it prepares you for whatever greater thing God has in your future. So don't think that you do not have a ministry gift. God has called every one of us to help advance His kingdom. Get involved wherever you are.

In addition to spiritual gifts, God also gives us natural gifts that are important to our future. For example, most of us played sports when we were young for enjoyment and exercise. There are a select few, however, who have a special talent that may enable them to earn a living in a certain sport. If you are a Christian and such a talent begins to emerge don't be afraid to pursue it. All of these gifts are God-given. We can either use it for our own selfish benefits or use it to give our lives purpose and be an influence for God.

God is looking for people who will represent His agenda in every field of endeavor including sport, arts, entertainment, business, commerce, politics, academia and science. If your destiny lies in any of these specialty areas, then you must be careful as the gift develops in you to remember that the purpose of the gift is to fulfill your destiny, and not to boost your ego. In 1 Corinthians 10:31, Paul reminds us that whatever we do, "do it all to the glory of God." Practicing this attitude will keep us out of trouble later on in life.

I want to touch briefly on careers and personal development. Sometimes we are not sure in what career direction the Lord wants us to go. You may be working in a job that you are not particularly happy with, but don't know if you should look for another job, change careers, go back to school, do additional training, or just stay where you are. How do we decide what to do?

I personally believe that God wants us to have meaningful, productive, *balanced* lives. What do I mean by a balanced life? What it does *not* mean is that we take a bit of God and a bit of what we want, and balance them together for our convenience.

A balanced Christian life is based on putting *God first* and what we want subject to His purpose. When we try to balance our own lives by finding slots for God, ministry, career, family and leisure, we often become unbalanced because we try to fit God into our busy schedules, and take on more of the other things that compete for our time and affections. This is why God said to seek Him first and all these things (family, ministry, career, leisure) will be added to you in proportions determined by Him. This is what will produce the balance you are looking for in life. Here's how this works in practice. Lets say you're not happy with your present job. You can do two things, start looking for a new job and leave the old one, or Seek God First (SGF).

We Seek God First by approaching Him in prayer: "Lord, You know that I am not happy with this job or career. Here are the things I don't like about it: it doesn't pay enough, my boss is mean and disrespectful, the hours are too long, it is not satisfying. I want to change, but I don't want to do so unless You want me to, so order my steps according to Your purpose. I submit myself to You and ask that if it is Your will that I move on, open the doors and show me the way out. If it is Your desire that I stay here for Your strategic purpose, show me what *I need to change* in my attitude or approach to this job, so that I can be at peace where I am. I place this in Your hands and trust You to lead me." However you verbalize this to God, if you take this attitude in prayer, you give Him the right of way (or you yield yourself) to accomplish His strategic agenda, which is what He wants from us all.

Sometimes the Lord will use our discomfort with where we are to move us on to another assignment. Other times, He wants us right where we are to either accomplish something for Him, or to change something in us. If we move before He is finished with us or accomplishes His purpose and releases us, then we step out of His will and plan. It is very important therefore that before we make any career change that we submit ourselves, and our motives to God, and allow Him to guide us.

The last bit of career advice I will offer is that we need to learn how to tune in to the voice of the Lord as He leads us. Jesus said that, "My sheep know my voice and they follow me" (John 10:27). The Lord speaks to us to provide direction in different ways. Sometimes He uses people to tell us what He wants of us and then confirms His direction in our spirit. At other times, it may be something we read in the word or hear in our hearts, or an incident that takes place in our lives. In order to follow the Lord we need to learn to distinguish between His voice and every other sound. The voice of logic and consensus is not necessarily the voice of God. Submit all advice you receive about your career potential, your skills and talents, and the direction you should pursue, to the standard of God's word and the confirmation of His Spirit. Not just because your counselor says that you would make a good lawyer you should automatically enroll in law school.

Also, don't give up if someone says that you do not

have the natural ability to achieve something that the Lord places on your heart, as His direction for you. If the Lord wants you in a particular career or to go in a specific direction, He will develop the necessary talents in you and equip you for His purpose, in spite of what anyone else may say about your lack of ability or experience. Learn to identify His voice in the midst of all the other sounds and noises you hear in life.

Get involved in God's strategic plan.

The walk of destiny requires us to work. In order to find our purpose in life we need to get involved in God's Strategic Plan for the world. To do this we need to prepare ourselves to explain to others, what God has done in our lives and what He can do in theirs. Paul told Timothy:

> Study to show yourself approved unto God, a worker who does not need to be ashamed, rightly dividing the word of truth.
> (2 Timothy 2:15)

Peter echoes this advice:

> But sanctify the Lord God in your hearts and always be ready to give a defense to everyone who asks you a reason for the hope that is in you, with meekness and fear.
> (1 Peter 3:15)

The message is crystal clear. God has invested a lot in His strategic plan and He is expecting us all to work with Him to make His salvation known to others. Yes, we have a hope of salvation and prospects of a divine destiny, but what about our neighbors and the other people with whom we come into contact? We have a responsibility to do two things:

- Study God's strategic plan and understand the word of truth (2 Timothy 2:15).

- Be available to give an answer to anyone who God would put in our path. (1 Peter 3:15).

You need to understand the scriptural basis of your salvation so you can explain it to others and help them find their destinies. Go through scripture and identify verses that speak about salvation, God's love, man's problem, reconciliation, forgiveness, etc. Read these Scriptures, understand them and commit them to memory. Ask someone who has an understanding of scripture to explain things to you that are not clear.

As you commit yourself to develop your understanding of God's plan of salvation, He will bring people in your path whom He is trying to reach. The conversation may start very casually, a comment, a question, a concern or a pleasant greeting.

When the Holy Spirit opens these doors our job is to be ready to share, not only our testimony of how God has helped us, but also to use God's word as the basis for what we say. This way it would not be you speaking to the person, but God using His word and your voice. If, however, we don't have God's word in us, then we will have very little to say and God cannot use us as He would want to.

Another way that we can be ready to "always give an answer" is to be a blessing wherever we go. There are many people that we meet in our day lives, on our jobs, in the community, who are weary and burdened by the cares of life, or who may be hurting, frustrated and in need. You never can tell when an opportunity will present itself to say a kind word, offer some advice or extend meaningful help. Sometimes little things make a big difference.

In addition, don't be timid when it comes to setting the right example. If, for example, your co-workers act disrespectfully to your employer or supervisor, shirk their responsibilities, waste time for which they are being paid, do sloppy work, and *you sit quietly by and endorse their behavior*, then you lose the opportunity to be a witness and testimony for God.

God expects us to be leaders wherever we go by setting the standard. It is not necessary to be in a position of authority to lead. Jesus said that we are the light of the world and the salt of the earth. You could be doing the most everyday ordinary task and people will follow the light that you shine and find a path to Christ. Our destiny is to be men and women of light.

Divine Destiny creates a legacy.

The walk of destiny creates our legacy. As parents we would all like to leave our children with some sort of financial inheritance, no matter how small. Maybe we will, maybe we won't. Much depends on factors over which we may have very little control. Recent history has shown how easy it is to lose your entire savings overnight.

But there is one legacy that we *can* leave, which is certain to survive us as parents.

> Train up a child in the way that he should go and when he is old he will not depart from it.
> (Proverbs 22:6)

The spiritual truths that you teach your children will be remembered and passed down from generation to generation long after their memory of you has faded. God's strategic plan changes lives and destinies for all eternity. As we play our part in promoting God's Kingdom, other people will come to understand and accept His plan for their lives. This is our privilege and legacy, the opportunity to work with God as agents of eternal change. Consider the legacy that the Apostle Paul left in the earth.

This truly remarkable man provides the greatest example of the impact of destiny in the life of any mortal man, in any field of endeavor. While his name is seldom mentioned among the literary greats his work lives on for all eternity.

All of the famous writers and philosophers in the world, such as Aristotle, Hemingway, Homer, Plato, Poe, Shakespeare, Twain and Voltaire, are easily recognized by name. Yet none of their works are as studied today as Paul's writings and letters are. Paul's letters are studied afresh all over the world, in homes, in churches and in universities by people of every walk of life, because the message he conveys *changes lives.*

God used Paul to execute His strategic plan by reaching out beyond the Jewish nation to people all over the world. His work was to explain salvation in a way that answers every question about who Jesus is and what He has done for us.

This is the power of destiny in God. Had Paul continued on the world's path, he probably would have been just another powerful Pharisee who lived and died two thousand years ago and who no one today remembers or even heard about. The important thing we learn from Paul's life and ministry is that it is not how we start, but how we finish the race.

Many of us have faced challenges in life. Some have experienced abuse, neglect or have had other trauma inflicted upon us. For others, the challenge could have been that we walked the wrong road at some time in our lives, both before and sometimes after we became Christians. Every one of us has a past, which is why we need forgiveness. Paul himself was a noted persecutor and executioner of Christians. Yet God was able to transform his life in a relatively short time and provide him with a glorious destiny. This is what God wants to do in each of us. No matter how we start, God wants us to finish strong. Here are some of Paul's last words before his execution:

> For I am already being poured out as a drink offering and the time of my departure is at hand. I have fought the good fight, I have finished the race, I have kept the faith. Finally, there is laid up for me a crown of righteousness which the Lord, the righteous Judge will give to me at that day, and not to me only, but also to all them who have loved his appearing.
> (2 Timothy 4:6-8)

Unbelievable! This is a man who knows that his execution is imminent, yet he sounds like he is preparing to attend the academy awards and to be awarded an Oscar. "I have fought a good fight, I have finished my course, I have kept the faith." Would that we can all say this when our time comes.

Don't expect the world to understand God's plan for you or to approve of your destiny in Him.
I am sure that those who knew Saul (later known as Paul) in the Jewish religious hierarchy would shake their heads and say, "Saul had such promise. Where did he go wrong?" From a career perspective, Paul had a bright future ahead of him. He is reported to have come from a reasonably wealthy family, was an outstanding scholar of Jewish law ("a Pharisee of Pharisees") and probably would have ended his career as a senior priest, if not chief priest. From the world's perspective

this young man was destined for great things as a respected, influential man of authority in Jewish society of the day.

That is, until God interrupted the world's plan for Paul and anointed him for a divine destiny. God's ways are not our ways. Sometimes the road that He chooses for us is not necessarily the one we would chose for ourselves, or the one that meets the approval of those around us. One of the signals that God sends us to confirm that we are following His plan for our lives, is a sense of divine peace in the midst of uncertainty.

It is important, therefore, not to always judge things by their natural outcome but to discern the leading and direction of the Spirit. There have been men and women who devoted their lives to some higher calling at the expense of living in comfort and safety. This may appear irrational to the natural man, but when God gives you the assurance that you are in His will and way, and that you are fulfilling your destiny in Him, no other consideration matters.

In everything give thanks

As we walk life's road towards God's destiny, we have to understand and accept, that not everything that crosses our path, will be to our liking. Sometimes the unexpected happens. We are walking in a particular direction, things are going great, and then suddenly, *everything changes.*

Some people handle change well. *Not me.* I like consistency, structure, and as much predictability as I can get in my life. Like the typical CPA, I like to see all my little ducks in a nice neat row. This is sometimes how I find myself thinking and praying: "Lord, please provide more certainty in my life. Make all the plans that I have for myself a reality, and keep me safe and secure in my comfort zone, Amen."

Good luck with that. Life is anything but predictable, and the walk of destiny often requires us to deal with change, so that we can be changed. God's plans for our lives may take us through unfamiliar terrain and uncertain paths, and His best for us may be to deliberately take us out of our comfort zones. He did it to Abraham, Moses and Paul, and He will to us as well. The greatest challenge for us is to remain calm in the midst of change and uncertainty, trusting that God will see us through. How do we do that? **By giving thanks.** As we look at the weather and see that storm approaching, we say "Lord, I don't know what You're doing, and I don't know where this is taking me, but I trust you. Thank you for your protection, covering and grace and for leading me according to Your strategic will and purpose."

As we practice this attitude of being thankful in spite of the circumstances, God gives us a sense of calm, an assurance of His presence, *and a boldness to command the storm to be still.*

> Oh give thanks to the Lord for He is good! For His mercy endures forever. Let the redeemed of the Lord say so, Whom He has redeemed from the hand of the enemy.
> (Psalm 107: 1-2)

Remember too, that the joy of the Lord is your strength (Nehemiah 8:10). These two, *thankfulness and joy*, go hand in hand. As we become thankful and grateful, the joy of the Lord arises in us, and gives us the strength to pursue our destiny, despite the obstacles.

Finally my brethren, be strong in the Lord and in the power of His might.

We have come to the end of this discussion of God's strategic plan. Hopefully the things that we have considered will help us all to not only understand God's plan for the world, but also to appreciate our value to Him, and the potential that is bound up in each of our lives. Writing this book has caused me to realize that, in spite of my successes and my failures so far, my destiny is still out there waiting to be fulfilled. So, it is up to me now to pick up the cross that I have avoided for so long, and start walking towards God's purpose for my life. *So must we all.*

May the Lord bless you and keep you; May He make His face to shine upon you and be gracious unto you. May He lift up His countenance upon you and grant you peace (Numbers 6:24-26).

Find your place in God's Strategic Plan and *fulfill your destiny!*

Robert.

NOTES

Chapter 1:

1) Online Business Dictionary:
(http://www.businessdictionary.com/definition/strategic-planning.html)

2) Origins of Strategic Planing: United Nations Educational Scientific and Cultural Organization: Strategic Planning: Concept and rationale:
(http://unesdoc.unesco.org/images/0018/001897/189757e.pdf)

3) Oxford Press Scholarship Online: Brief History of Business Strategy:
(http://www.oxfordscholarship.com/view/10.1093/019828988X.001.0001
/acprof-9780198289883-chapter-21)

Chapter 2

1) Sun Tzu Biography, Society for the Recognition of Famous People:
(http://www.thefamouspeople.com/profiles/sun-tzu-261.php)

2) Ancient History Encyclopedia: (http://www.ancient.eu.com/Sun-Tzu/)

Chapter 3

The Higgs Boson: What You Should Know About What It Is And What It Does: Ainissa Rameriez, Yale University:
(http://www.forbes.com/sites/allenstjohn/2012/07/09/the-higgs-boson-
what-you-should-know-about-what-it-is-and-what-it-does/)

Chapter 4:

Biological Altruism: Stanford Encyclopedia of Philosophy:
(http://plato.stanford.edu/entries/altruism-biological/)

Chapter 5

The Jewish Virtual Library; The Holocaust: An Introductory History:
(http://www.jewishvirtuallibrary.org/jsource/Holocaust/history.html)

Chapter 6

Federal Bureau of Investigation; FBI Ten Most Wanted Fugitive: Osama Bin
Laden: (http://www.fbi.gov/wanted/topten/usama-bin-laden)

Chapter 7:

Bible Hermeneutics: What is the scroll of Revelation 5:8?
(http://hermeneutics.stackexchange.com/questions/6129/what-is-on-the-
sealed-scroll-in-revelation-5-8)

Chapter 9:

Supreme art of war: Brainy Quotes
(http://www.brainyquote.com/quotes/authors/s/sun_tzu.html)

Chapter 12:

1) The Top Tens: Best Forest Gump quotes:
(http://www.thetoptens.com/best-forrest-gump-quotes/)

2) Song facts Que Sera, Sera:(http://www.songfacts.com/detail.php?
id=4667)

3) Andrew Carnegie: (http://carnegie.org/about-us/foundation-
history/about-andrew-carnegie/)

4) But They Did Not Give Up: Henry Ford:
(http://www.uky.edu/~eushe2/Pajares/OnFailingG.html)

5) Lean In: Ursula Burns: (http://leanin.org/stories/ursula-burns/)

6) Goodreads: Quotes about destiny:
(http://www.goodreads.com/quotes/tag/destiny)

ABOUT THE AUTHOR

Robert V. Fullerton is a Georgia licensed Certified Public Accountant, a Fellow of the Association of Chartered Certified Accountant UK, and holds an MBA from the Heriot Watt University, Scotland.

He is a seasoned business professional with over 25 years experience in public accounting and as a CFO, CEO, and Business Consultant. He provides consultancy services in the areas of Financial Management and Strategic Planning to owner managed businesses, and serves on the Board of Directors and Management Committees of client entities.

Robert accepted the Lord Jesus as his Savior some 30 years ago, and has been active in youth ministry, as a church board member, and conference speaker. He conducts seminars and workshops on Biblical financial planning and works closely with Christian business-owners to help them manage their businesses on the basis of sound financial and Biblical principles.

Robert is originally from Trinidad and Tobago and has been married to Jacqueline for 25 years. They live in Buford, GA. and have three children, Jesse, Chloe, and Caitlin.

ROBERT SPEAKS ON:

"Biblical Strategies for Finances"

God is strategic and His word is a source of guidance on every aspect of our lives, *including our finances*. We, however, often "perish for a lack of knowledge" because we don't access God's wisdom, and apply His principles as the basis for our financial dealings.

This results in us either making poor decisions which affect our lives, or missing opportunities to lay hold of what God really wants for us.

Here are some of Robert's speaking topics on Biblical strategies for finances:

Family and Personal Finances

1) Personal Financial Planning Based on Biblical Principles:
- Practical and Biblical advice for dealing with personal finances.

2) "Debt...the snare of the fowler": - Should I get in? How Do I get out?

3) "Two become one": - Advice for husbands and wives (and those thinking about getting married).

<u>Business Transformation Based on Biblical Principles:</u>

1) "Grow your business God's way": How to Create sustainable business value and impose financial discipline on your business.

2) Five Strategies of successful Christian Business Owners: Your business, your ministry. How to pursue God's Strategic Agenda for your business.

3) School of Business for Christian Entrepreneurs: A combination of Biblical principles and practical management training for **Christian Business Owners**. (Topics include: Christian Business Ethics and Governance; Financial and Strategic management *simplified*; Entity selection; Accounting, Taxes and Legal issues for small business owners; and others).

For further information please contact:

Robert V. Fullerton, CPA.
Email: rfullerton@christiancfo.com

Websites: www.rvfcfo.com
www.christiancfo.com

Made in the USA
Middletown, DE
02 May 2015